What

Conscious

BOOK TWO

Darlene is one of those special people who can truly inspire others. Her stories are very rare, kind, sincere, and beloved. You may get "tearbugs" or find yourself in a fit of laughter. But in the end, you will feel better and stronger.

~ Julie Isphording, NPR Radio Talk Show Host and Producer

Conscious Women – Conscious Lives Book Two wakes up the heart to what is true and important in life. A wonderful and heartwarming collection that is worth reading.

~Melvina Walter, Executive Director, The Women's Centre

You will laugh, cry, learn and grow, and most of all, the deepest part of your soul will connect powerfully with the universal wisdom and love that is woven throughout this book and found in the fabric of each and every story. *Conscious Women – Conscious Lives Book Two* is a book that honors and celebrates life in all its shades and forms … Thank you, Darlene Montgomery, for bringing this gift to us!

~ Jill Hewlett, Host, Body, Mind, and Spirit Television

Conscious Women – Conscious Lives Book Two is a potent tribute to the amazing ability of women to rise out of extraordinary circumstances and reinvent themselves. These stories prove that miracles are alive today in ordinary people's lives.

~ Heather Thompson, News Director/Radio Host, 105.9 Jack FM

An extraordinary series of stories! *Conscious Women – Conscious Lives Book Two* is a modern account of how legacies are created in ordinary women's lives.

~ Janet Matthews, Author, Inspirational Speaker
Co-author, *Chicken Soup for the Canadian Soul*

Darlene's collection of stories will lead you gently through the barrier of fear to the pathway of hope. I felt the healing experience of each woman as she held her fear and trusted. These remarkable women remind us about our own Goddess within and how we can inspire our future from love and peace instead of fear. What a wonderful book! It lightened my heart.

~ Colleen Hoffman Smith, author of *Pocket Guide to Your Heart* and *Pocket Guide to Your Heart for Relationships*

As we feel the pain, the joy, and the insights of these remarkable stories, inevitably we relate to our own life experience and take up the implied invitation to reflect on what is truly important to us. They say that stories are the healing breath of our ancestors. Here is a book that is the healing breath of unmet friends.

~ Fay Wilkinson, An Illisaiji of Expressive Arts

Conscious Women – Conscious Lives

BOOK TWO

Conscious Women – Conscious Lives

BOOK TWO

Darlene Montgomery

From the Social Issues Series:
White Knight's Remarkable Women

White Knight Publications
Toronto, Canada

Copyright © 2005 by Darlene Montgomery

All rights reserved. The use of any part of this publication reproduced, transmitted in any form or by any means, electronic, mechanical, photocopying, recording, or otherwise, or stored in a retrieval system, without the prior written consent of The Publisher – or, in the case of photocopying or other reprographic copying, a license from the Canadian Copyright Licensing Agency – is an infringement of the copyright law.

Published in 2005 by
White Knight Publications, a division of Bill Belfontaine Ltd.
Suite 103, One Benvenuto Place, Toronto Ontario Canada M4V 2L1
T. 416-925-6458 F, 416-925-4165 • e-mail whitekn@istar.ca

Ordering information

CANADA
Hushion House Publishing Inc.
c/o Georgetown Terminal Warehouses
34 Armstrong Avenue,
Georgetown ON, L7G 4R9
T:1-866-485-5556 F:1-866-485-6665

UNITED STATES
Hushion House Publishing Inc.
c/o Stackpole Distribution
7253 Grayson Road
Harrisburg PA, 17111 USA
T:1-888-408-0301 F: 1-717-564-8307

First printing: May 2005

National Library of Canada Cataloguing in Publication
    Conscious women – conscious lives / Darlene Montgomery, editor.
    ISBN 0-9734186-1-3 (bk. 1).-ISBN 0-9736705-0-9 (bk. 2)
    1. Self-help techniques. 2. Women.
    I. Montgomery, Darlene, 1958-
    BF632.C65 2004   158.1   C2004-900381-X

Cover Art: "Road to the River" © 2003 Mary Carroll Moore
Cover and Text Design: Karen Petherick, Intuitive Design International Ltd.
Edited by Laura Reave
"Coming Home to Oz" edited by Shelley Hyndman
Printed and Bound in Canada

Permissions:
"Healing My Perceptions," by Marianne Williamson from A Return to Love by Marianne Williamson, pages 202-206 Copyright ©1992 by Marianne Williamson. Portions reprinted from A COURSE IN MIRACLES copyright © 1975 by Foundation for Inner Peace Inc. All chapter openings are from A COURSE IN MIRACLES.

"The Emperor's New Clothes" by Rachel Remen, M.D., from KITCHEN TABLE WISDOM by Rachel Naomi Remen, M.D., pages 93-99. Copyright © 1996 by Rachel Naomi Remen, M.D. Used by permission of Riverhead Books, an imprint of Penguin Group (USA) Inc. Permissions continued page 190.

Contents

Dedication

To Lily,

for your strength and determination

Acknowledgements

Thanks to Jean Versteeg, my "publicist," for leading me to some wonderful women with wonderful stories to share. Thanks to Marlene Chapelle, Eva Lemster, Yolande Savoie, Barb Russo-Smith, Lily Bedikian, Jane and Paul Pulkys, Janet Matthews, Kathryn Drayton, Shelley Hyndman, Lily Bedikian, Carol Lidstone, Janet Matthews, and other friends who provided loving support along the way. I thank you with all my heart.

Thanks to Deborah Davis and Katie Alexander for delving deeper to write their stories. You showed great courage in revealing yourself so that others could gain from your experiences.

Thanks to Barb Allport for your willingness to write again about such a personal journey of healing and transformation. Thanks to Naomi Remen for your generosity in allowing your wonderful story to be a part of this book.

Thanks to all of you who wrote to say how much *Conscious Women Book One* had touched your lives.

Thanks to Heather Thompson at Jack FM for being an amazing inspiration to me and to others as you serve life with your beautiful heart.

Thanks to Erin Davis for spreading the word about *Conscious Women Book One* and for contributing again to *Conscious Women Book Two*. You really walk the talk!

Thanks to my Mom, who keeps on going strong even though Parkinson's has tried to keep you from doing so.

Thanks to my beautiful daughter Jessica, who at such a young age demonstrates both wisdom and charity.

Thanks to Bill Belfontaine for your incredible spirit that drives you to create wonderful books and for your support of me through these years as a writer and friend.

Thanks to Karen Petherick for your creative work on the book and for your spiritual insights along the way.

Thanks to each of you from my heart who gave your time to conceive your idea and then invest your emotions, love, and often tears to give birth to your story.

Thank you to each and every one who became a participant in creating this book.

And a special thanks to Sri Harold Klemp, who has kept his promise and who is always with me as teacher, friend, and guide.

~ *Darlene Montgomery*

Introduction

One of the most valuable things we can do to heal one
another is listen to each other's stories.
– Rebecca Falls

Our stories are what hold this world together. As a child I read
stories and parables that taught me deep truths. I went from
book to book, searching for some eternal truth to satisfy my
inner yearnings. From as early as the age of seven, I knew one
day I would share my own stories with others and that my
stories were somehow part of how the eternal part of each of
us has expression. Our experiences temper us and shape us
into the vessels that God uses to mirror truth to others.

In compiling these stories from women's rich experiences, I learned that illness, adversity, and change are not
things to fear, but gifts that burn out of us our limitations and
inadequacies to expose the diamond of our true self. Along
the way, I heard from women how the writing of their stories
was therapeutic and brought completion and resolution to
their journeys.

Conscious Women Book Two came by request from those
who read the first *Conscious Women – Conscious Lives* and
expressed a yearning for more of these heartfelt stories that
reveal our deepest struggles and our greatest victories.

Together we can triumph over our most difficult circumstances, learning to trust as children in the source of life, and
together we can find the will and inner strength to follow our
dreams and fulfill our greatest destiny. It is through the bond

we share with those who truly love and believe in us that we are released from the illusion of our mortality and connected with the truth of our immortality.

In the words of the narrator from the movie *Big Fish*, "If we share our stories long enough, we become our stories, and in becoming our stories we are immortal."

These stories are from all of us to all of you with love.

~ *Darlene Montgomery*

Healing Journeys

All healing is essentially the release from fear.

– A Course in Miracles

Life is a Gift

Just before my fifteenth birthday, I moved with my family from Fort William, in the Highlands of Scotland, to the town of Paisley in Renfrewshire. Because my dad was a United Free Church Minister, our new home was a large granite house that had been built in the early 1820s to accommodate the clergy.

Although I loved this old Victorian home during the daylight hours, it could seem quite spooky as soon as dusk began to fall. If my parents were out for the evening, passersby could be sure to see a light coming from every room in the house, as well as hear the loud blaring of our wartime radio. I was so afraid of the dark, especially at bedtime!

One way around this was to imagine a circle of protective angel wings surrounding my bed at night while repeating, "Four good angels guard my bed, one at the foot and one at the head, one on the left and one on the right, guarding me throughout the night."

Thankfully, my bedroom used to be the maid's room, so it was smaller and cozier than the others. The kitchen was my favourite room in the house because it was a reflection of my mother's warm and cheerful ways, and there was always a wonderful aroma of home-cooked meals in the air. This is where the whole family congregated to eat in front of a large coal fire that seemed to burn endlessly from early morning until late at night.

To earn some pocket money, my brother and I worked on

weekends for Mr. Angus MacMillan in his store "Galbraith's." I was often put in charge of the bakery department, but on several occasions, I was asked to run some errands on my bike for my manager.

One day, as I sped along to deliver an important message, my bike wheel got caught on one of the tramcar lines, and I was thrown directly in front of a fast-moving double-decker bus. My life flashed before me as the bus wheel approached my head. I knew that I couldn't possibly hope to survive for more than a few seconds. As death stared me in the face, I remembered my dad's favourite saying: "Let go and let God."

All I could do now was to surrender to a power greater than myself. For an agonizing moment, time seemed to stand still. Then out of nowhere, the figure of a man miraculously appeared with outstretched arms to hold back the bus. I thought, surely I must be dreaming! Yet the bus screeched to a halt about an inch from my head! When my head hit the cobblestone, I was temporarily dazed, and because I was in a state of shock, I seemed to be seeing in black and white. The figure towering above me appeared to be in his thirties and gave the impression of being very tall and muscular. He wore a short robe tied at the waist and had black hair and a short beard. Then the mysterious stranger vanished as quickly as he appeared, and I was left to marvel that not even a single hair on my head had been touched. Someone up there loved me very much!

Judging from the circle of white faces staring at me in disbelief, I knew that we had all just witnessed a miracle! Why was MY life so important that I had been given another chance? Who was this mysterious guardian angel? He certainly looked different from the angels I envisioned every night.

As I got to my feet, gratitude filled my heart, and I knew that there must be some purpose to my life. That night, as I drifted off to sleep, I was surrounded by a blazing sheet of pure white light. I felt very loved and cared for as I entered my dream world. A man with twinkling blue eyes and a warm smile appeared to me out of the light. He was wearing a pale blue suit and appeared to be a man in his forties with brown hair and a pleasant, round face. (No wings!) He said that he would be my spiritual guide, and for an entire week he appeared nightly in the same blazing light to teach me in some way.

One night he came to help me overcome my fear of death by showing me that life continues on after the death of the physical body. A small, red-haired, three-year-old boy had just died, and so my guide and I took him by the hand and led him lovingly into the spirit world on the other side. The love that I experienced that night was incredible. I learned that the real me, "my inner self," lives on forever. In the morning I rushed downstairs to the kitchen to share my dream experiences with my dad.

As I was telling him about the little red-haired boy, the telephone in the hall began to ring, and he left me for a moment to answer it. A very distraught father, sobbing quietly on the other end of the line, begged my dad to lead a funeral for his little three-year-old son. Apparently he wasn't affiliated with any particular church, and so my dad agreed to lead the funeral service.

"That's the same little boy I helped last night!" I announced to my dad. "Can I go to the funeral to tell the parents that their little boy is OK?"

"No," my dad said, much to my great disappointment. "They wouldn't believe you. They would think you were crazy."

My spiritual guide continued to appear sporadically in my dreams from 1956 to 1971. Over this span of 15 years, by helping me to overcome my fear of death, he also helped me to overcome my fear of life. He showed me that my purpose for being here was to learn all that I could about unconditional love so that one day I could be of service to life.

Life is a gift. Embrace it with LOVE.

~ *Sybil Barbour*

Once at Big Lake

When I was little I knew the woods well,
knew the narrow foot paths
through golden sweep of field
and over ancient rock fences,
paths through the forest so covered with damp leaves
that I thought, like Hansel and Gretel,
I should leave a trail to follow,
but I always found my way.
Paths to Big Lake and paths to Frog Pond,
paths only children knew,
while the grown-ups took their cars
if they ever came at all
to the places we played,
secret places, and secret paths.
Some, it seemed, I alone knew,
to seek out my own alone time,
to dangle my feet from the edge of the dam,
and gaze, pensive, into the water.
Once in my peaceful reverie
I imagined an Indian brave
who stood on the embankment,
and spoke to my Soul, gently,
and I answered, quietly,
still gazing at the sun-lit water,
afraid to look up and break the spell,
until the presence became so real,
I jumped to my feet and turned and ran,
panting, heart pounding, not caring

the branches and thorns
catching at my clothes, scratching the bare skin.
I knew only that I had wandered into
some great mystery, maybe more
than a childish fantasy, maybe more
than I could ever make up,
and suddenly the home I had sought to escape
looked so comforting and familiar
that I was glad, for a while,
to be back, and to forget, for a while,
the Mystery that stood waiting
on the other side of the stream.

~ *Laura Reave*

Healing My Perceptions

A human being is part of a whole, called by us the
'Universe,' a part limited in time and space. He experiences
himself, his thoughts and feelings, as something separated
from the rest – a kind of optical delusion of his consciousness. This delusion is a kind of prison for us, restricting us
to our personal desires and to affection for a few persons
nearest us. Our task must be to free ourselves from this
prison by widening our circles of compassion to embrace all
living creatures and the whole of nature in its beauty.
- Albert Einstein

Several years ago, when I had just begun lecturing on A
Course in Miracles, I had a series of three car accidents in
which I was rear-ended on the freeway. In every case, I had
surrendered the experience immediately, remembering that I
was not subject to the effect of worldly danger, and was not
harmed or hurt in any way.

A week or so after the last accident, I developed a cold
and a serious sore throat. On a Friday afternoon, with a
lecture to give about the Course the next morning, I was feeling terrible. I had a date for drinks after work with my
girlfriend Sarah. Since I felt so bad, I wanted to cancel the
date and go home to bed, but when I called Sarah's office, I
was told that she had already left for the day. I had no choice
but to go to the café, and on my way driving there, I turned
my attention to healing my throat. I wished desperately for
access to a doctor, because I knew that an antibiotic called

Erythromycin had always healed this throat problem for me in the past. Since I was new in Los Angeles, I didn't know any doctors. I turned to the Course. How did this happen? I asked myself. Where did my thinking deviate from truth? Where was my wrong-minded perception? I received an answer as soon as I asked, and it struck me like a bolt of lightning. Although I had applied principles in relation to the accident itself, I had "given into temptation" right afterwards. In what way?

After three accidents, everyone I knew had come up to ask if I was all right. They put their hands on me, rubbed my neck and back gently, inquired as to whether I had seen a doctor, and oozed gentleness all over me. The attention felt good. Being sick made people love me more. Instead of responding with a full tilt, "I'm fine," the "I'm fine" came out a little more timidly, lest they'd stop rubbing my neck. I had bought into – entered into agreement with – the idea of my physical vulnerability in order to receive the payoff of love and attention.

I paid a high price for my "sin," i.e., loveless perception. My perception was wrong-minded in the sense that I saw myself as a body rather than a spirit, which is loveless rather than loving self-identification. Choosing to believe I was vulnerable, even for an instant, made me so. Thus my sore throat.

Great! I thought. I got it! "God," I said, "I totally understand how this happened. I return my mind to the point of my error, and I atone. I go back. I ask that my perception be healed, and I ask to be released from the effects of my wrong-minded thinking. Amen." I closed my eyes at a red light while I said the prayer, and fully expected to be free of my sore throat when I opened them again.

The prayer over, I opened my eyes. My throat still hurt. This wasn't supposed to happen. Now more depressed than ever, I went into the café where I was to meet my friend and took a seat at the bar. I noticed as I entered that there was a man at the other end of the bar, looking at me in a flirtatious kind of way. He was anything but my type. I looked at him as though to say, "One more look in my direction, buddy, and you're dead."

"Can I help you?" asked the bartender.

"Yes," I whispered hoarsely. "I want some brandy, some honey, and some milk."

The man at the other end of the bar watched as the bartender returned with the items I'd requested. "What are you trying to do?" he asked.

I did not want to speak to this man. I wanted him to go away. But once the Course has gotten into your system, you never again have guilt-free bitchy thoughts. "He's your brother, Marianne," I said to myself. "He's an innocent child of God. *Be nice.*"

I softened. "I'm trying to make a hot toddy," I said. "I have a very bad sore throat."

"Well, first of all, that's not the way to make a hot toddy," he said, "and secondly, that's not what you want anyway. You probably need some penicillin."

"That's true, I do," I said, "Erythromycin would cure this, but I just moved to L.A., and I don't know any doctors who would prescribe it to me."

The man got up and walked over to where I was sitting. He put a credit card on the bar and beckoned the bartender. "Come on, let's go next door," he said to me. "I can get some Erythromycin."

I looked at him like he was crazy, but I also noticed that the credit card said, "Dr." on it. "What's next door?" I asked.

"A Thrifty drugstore."

And so it was. We walked next door to Thrifty, and my new friend the doctor prescribed the medicine I wanted. After throwing one pill into my mouth, I became ecstatic.

"You don't understand," I said to him, practically jumping up and down. "This is a miracle! I prayed for healing, and I corrected my thoughts, but the Holy Spirit couldn't give me an instantaneous healing because I'm not advanced enough yet to receive it – it would be too threatening to my belief system – so He had to enter at the level of my understanding, and you were there! But if I hadn't opened my heart to you, I would never have been able to receive the miracle because I wouldn't have been open!"

He handed me his business card. "Young lady, here's my number," he said. "I'm a psychiatrist, and I haven't prescribed an antibiotic in twenty-five years. But trust me, you should give me a call."

~Marianne Williamson

This personal email letter was sent to the author by her dear friend Arlene Forbes as a follow-up of a letter published in *Conscious Women Book One*.

A Circle of Friends

Part 2

Hi All:

It's been a week since my surgery, and I am home sweet home. In an act of true surrender and trust, I gave the doctor permission to perform the surgery according to what she found inside me.

The result was a partial hysterectomy on December 5. My ovaries, fallopian tubes, and cervix were in good enough shape to be left in place. The really great thing is that I don't have to worry about hormone replacement therapy (HRT) and all the controversy. Of course there were surprises, which I will get into later.

It is always a plus to have the guidance of Divine Spirit on your side. I got the nudge to do two things before the operation: 1) Go check out the hospital before surgery, and 2) Go see the doctor with any last-minute questions. At the hospital the staff nurses engaged in friendly banter and reassured me of good care. The environment was very clean, professional, and welcoming.

This was a great way to spiritually prepare myself and nip any fears in the bud before surgery. It was also a way to let them know a member of the Forbes clan would be there in a week's time. I had five questions for the doctor, but I only had to ask the first question, since her answer covered all the other questions. Everything was in Divine order, I thought. She then said of all the hysterectomies she has performed, this one would be an honor. I had resisted having surgery for five years.

I was reassured in so many ways that all would be well, and this was the right thing to do. The night before surgery I did a spiritual exercise and found myself in a dome-shaped room lying on a table surrounded by five beings dressed in white surgical scrubs and masks. My abdomen was huge, as if I was pregnant. My doctor came in and gave me a nod; another said that I would be 'just fine.' I also saw several paintings on the surrounding wall that on close inspection were pictures of several incomplete projects I had started. Then a brilliant light shone on my abdomen, and it became flat.

I awoke with a good feeling about the events about to unfold. Another reassurance for me was that all five traffic lights on the way to the hospital were green.

Dr. Christiane Northrop's book on menopause was very helpful in bringing me to an understanding of how women sometimes misdirect their creative energies and how this may create fibroids in their bodies (read p. 242). I highly recommend it.

On the day of the surgery, I had great support and love from my husband and friends. I could not be more grateful to them, especially for being there at 5:30 a.m. Other good news was that my hemoglobin blood count was 14, compared to 4.5 in February when I had to get a transfusion. Normal count is 12.5 to 14. It could not get any better than this. In the operating room all I remember is going into a bright white light as a CD recording of many people singing HU, an ancient name for God, played in the background.

A little over two hours later, I awoke in pain, foggy from the anesthesia. My husband gave me the good news. I am not quite clear about this memory, but I was told that a few minutes later I sang "Haven't Got Time for the Pain" with three of my girlfriends.

Later my husband explained the surprise the doctor

found. One of the fibroids was growing outside the uterus, and it lay on top of my bladder, bruising and irritating it. This would have caused problems later on if it were not removed. What a relief and a blessing!

On the first night I hardly got any sleep, and by the next day my exhaustion had built up into irritation. A very kind nurse was nice enough to listen and take action. She put me in a room by myself so I got a great night's sleep.

Post surgery has been filled with much love from my circle of friends. They have supported my healing journey by spending 'love' time with me, cooking with love for me, sending cards and flowers of love, bringing bottled water, and calling with get-well wishes. Thanks especially to my sister Linda for her loving vigilance and protection of the healing space required for a speedy recovery. I continue to have the courage to move forward with my healing, thanks to my daughters, who actually thanked *me* for taking the opportunity to love and heal myself.

~ *Love, Arlene*

The Road Less Traveled

Do not follow where the path may lead.
Go instead where there is no path and leave a trail.
- Ralph Waldo Emerson

As I stood before my brother's coffin, wanting so desperately to understand why he had taken his life, I made a promise to him that his death would not be in vain. Standing there, weeping in disbelief, I made a vow to my eight-year-old son David that he would not inherit the legacy of alcoholism that had brought so much grief to my family, my brother, and myself.

I was born in the small mining town of Timmins, Ontario, in the spring of 1952, the first of five children. In the late fall of 1953, I was still too young to know that my father was a chronic alcoholic and that my mother, at her wit's end, had decided to take me and leave my father. She presented him with an ultimatum: Stop drinking or we are gone. Not wanting to lose his precious baby girl, he quit drinking and joined the fellowship of Alcoholics Anonymous. Our home became an unofficial treatment center, our lives revolving around alcoholics and Alcoholics Anonymous.

And so my life was a series of mishaps and misfortunes, highlighted by sexual abuse and addiction. Finally, at eighteen years old, I left my family and moved to North Bay to attend college. While there, I met Fred, who was stationed in North Bay with the armed forces. I was in love for the first time, so desperately in love. Fred and I were married on June

29, 1974, and two years later on January 7, 1976, our only son David was born.

Children learn what they live, and I didn't want my son to grow up the way I had, so about five years into the marriage I started going to Alcoholics Anonymous. My mom was drinking very heavily at the time, and it was taking a tremendous toll on the emotional and mental health of our family, individually and collectively. I didn't want to have this legacy of alcoholism continue for another generation. It had already gone on for four, if not five, generations.

On June 29, 1984, our ninth wedding anniversary, I went strawberry picking with David in the morning and then to the Gatineau Hills for a picnic and swimming. It was a beautiful sunny day, and I felt incredibly blessed and lucky to be alive. We arrived home at 4 p.m. to a call from my brother Jim who'd apparently been trying to reach me all day. He was hysterical as he said, "Dougie's dead! He's committed suicide!" I thought, 'Stop it. That's not funny.' Douglas was only seventeen, a very gentle soul and more like a son to me than a brother.

Douglas's death acted like an atomic bomb on my family. There was fallout everywhere. Up until Douglas's death, my sheer willpower had kept my marriage together. Now, when I was forced to deal with my real feelings, my marriage began to fall apart.

After the funeral, I recognized the signs that I was headed for a drinking binge, so I entered St. Joseph's Drug and Alcohol Treatment Centre, while Fred, who had returned from Alert, where he was stationed in the Northwest Territories, stayed to look after David. Intensive treatment began as I really started to understand how alcoholism had held me captive.

After I completed my treatment, I returned home to my life, still extremely fragile. But then, six months later, we were posted across Canada to Calgary, a place where I knew no one. I was drowning in grief and looking for a sign from God.

On Pentecostal Sunday, as I sat in church looking up at the banner of the dove of Pentecost, everything seemed to vaporize except the DOVE – no more people or church or pews. Then to my surprise a voice inside me clearly said, "You must leave your marriage!"

I recoiled at the words and said, "No! I can't – it's too much to ask of me." I'd known for some time that my marriage was in trouble, but I thought with just a bit more time and effort I could make it work.

The voice was insistent. "You must leave your marriage!"

I said I would agree but that HE, the voice, would have to promise to change me because I knew that if I stayed the same, I would repeat the same mistakes. I left church completely devastated.

All that day I cried, until I could cry no longer. Not knowing what to do, Fred went out and took David with him. By the time he returned, I had gained the strength to tell him that I had to leave the marriage. The next day I bought two airplane tickets for David and myself to leave in one week for Ottawa, where I had an AA sponsor I trusted and an AA network of meetings and friends.

At the end of the week, when it was time to leave, I had the heart-wrenching task of explaining to our eight-year-old son what was to happen. Sitting on the rocking chair, I placed David on my lap. Looking into his innocent face, I told him how much Mommy and Daddy loved him, but that Deborah and Fred didn't get along any more, and that I was going back to Ottawa. I told him it was up to him and that he could choose to stay with whomever he wanted. Afterward I regretted giving him that choice. Next came the terrible words: "I am staying with my Daddy." It came as a total shock that my little boy wouldn't be coming to live with me!

I left the house with Fred and David crying on the sidewalk. Stunned and in shock, I somehow got myself to the airport to catch my flight. Sitting on the plane, I kept waiting for someone to sit down beside me, but then I would remember that David wouldn't be accompanying me.

I finally arrived in Ottawa, where a friend from AA was waiting at the airport. Seeing I was alone, she asked, "Where is David?" Again the shock hit me: "My baby is gone."

For the next three months I stayed with a generous AA family to begin my healing. For the first while, I cried, took walks, and went to meetings, just trying to make sense of all that I was feeling. At times, on my walks, my knees would buckle as I collapsed from the weight of my sorrow.

As I progressed in my healing, I moved out of my friend's home, first into one room in a home, and then into a basement apartment. That first summer David visited me. I was so happy to see my little boy. But as the years passed, opportunities to see my son were fewer and fewer.

For the first two years I had minimum-wage-paying jobs waiting tables, bussing tables, and working for a medical lab. With the funds from my work, I started accumulating enough to have basic furniture. At one point I decided to apply for a security job. As part of the process I had to have my fingerprints taken at the police station. While there I heard my inner voice say, "Go apply for dispatch." That made sense to me because I'd worked as a switchboard operator for the Canadian Embassy in Washington, D.C., from 1976 to 1979, when my husband was posted there with the Armed Forces.

The dispatch position was designated as a bilingual job, so when I asked for an application form, the Human Resources officer refused after learning that I didn't speak French. "Who's looking out for us Englishmen?" I spoke up with resolve, in a way completely out of character for me.

It seemed to have the right effect, because the man happened to have a thick British accent, and he brought me into his office and handed me an application for Special Constable, a position that had been brought into existence in 1984. To my amazement and excitement, out of 1500 applicants, I was one of only nine hired! And although I was afraid of confrontation, I took the job. I knew in my heart that the God of my understanding wanted me in this job for a reason.

Just before I was hired on the police force, I joined a wonderful religion called Eckankar that taught about divine love and how to master one's own destiny. With tip money from my job waiting tables, I saved enough to fly to Atlanta, Georgia, where there was an Eckankar seminar – a congregation of over 5,000 people coming together for spiritual renewal. This was to be a turning point in my healing.

While standing on a bridge in Atlanta, I was crying, as I had been doing for a very long time. A woman just passing by stopped and came over to comfort me. I learned she was also a member of Eckankar and coincidentally lived in Ottawa too. This was a meeting soul to soul.

After I returned home, my new friend Jean would call me on the phone to say hello. For many years I never called her back, but that never deterred her from calling to ask how I was and to offer words of encouragement and love.

Jean would call and say, "Deb, I just want you to know that I care. Call me back if you want – just know it's OK if you don't." Over the years a bond of trust grew between us, and I started to return her calls. I had finally met someone who loved me unconditionally and never withdrew her love. She broadened my horizons by introducing me to creative people who were spiritual, knowledgeable, and expansive. Jean was my lifeline. She always made sure that I didn't stay under too long.

Jean was also instrumental in introducing me to a psychiatrist who opened up a whole new world for me. Through him I got the medication I needed that changed the color of my world from dull gray to all colors of the rainbow. After two years of seeing him, I had also lost an extra fifty pounds I'd carried most of my life. I was finally letting down my defenses.

Last week I had a dinner party, the first one since my brother's death twenty years ago. I held the party in my own home with freshly painted walls, a new rug and curtains, great food, and wonderful friends. A new cycle has begun for me where I am truly experiencing myself as a person worthy of love, joy, and happiness.

My son David has grown into a wonderful, well-adjusted man, and he has come to understand why I chose to leave those many years ago. Seeing him grow has helped me realize that I made the right choice. David has found the love of his life, and I'll be flying out to be present when he says his wedding vows next spring. A big part of my healing came when I read this wonderful letter he wrote to me as a Christmas gift last year.

Dear Mom,

Forgiveness seems to be a trivial thing sometimes, but it is the basis of true unconditional love. I know that only the individual can be responsible for his own feelings. I understand that you must love yourself before you can truly and totally love another. I did not, however, know this from the beginning. It was handed down to me, as are all great bits of wisdom. My teacher is the incredible person I have the honor of calling my mother, who through her own trials and tribulations came to these same realizations.

I look at myself today, and think of where I am, and I can honestly say that I do not think that I would be here if it were not for Deborah Davis, my mom. I have her to thank for my respect for women, for my willingness to take the more difficult route, for my not being afraid to express myself to an individual for whom I care, and for the stubbornness to never quit. If only Deborah could look at me, the wonderful individual she says I am, and realize that it is only because of her that I possess many of these qualities.

Love,
David Russell

These gifts are the light to the shadow side of my life. I kept my promise to myself and to David. I took the road less traveled, and for that I am forever grateful!

~ *Deborah Davis*

Starting to Choose

Personal mastery teaches us to choose. Choosing is a
courageous act: picking the results and actions which you
will make into your destiny.
— Peter Senge

"You do have choices," he said.

I was sitting on the other side of the desk from my psychiatrist, the man I came to see twice a week. Just the week before, he had phoned me in the morning when I missed my appointment.

"Georgina, where are you?"

"I'm in bed. I can't seem to get up."

"Have you been to the bathroom yet?"

"No, and I have to go, but I can't seem to manage my body. It doesn't want to move."

"OK, I'll hang up the phone. You go to the bathroom, and call me when you get back to the bedroom."

This wonderful doctor had done this process a few times over the past five months, each time talking me gently into re-entering the day. Today, as I faced him, my arms, back and face were covered with small, itchy red spots. Shingles. These shingles appeared every time a letter from my mother in England plopped through the letterbox. Even before I knew the content of the letter, old memories of brutal beatings, of my body being thrown down the staircase, and my head being banged against the wall flooded my mind and body.

On the surface, everything had looked great. I was in my

teens, working as a relief receptionist, travelling to and from the small-town flat we lived in to go to an office in London. But my clothes hid the bruises. My smile hid the pain. And worst of all, I had no idea I had any choice. I was terrified of her. And had been for as long as I could remember. She had convinced me that she 'knew' what I was doing at all times, wherever I was.

In addition, the clothes I wore, the food I ate, the music I listened to, even the books or newspapers I read were all chosen by her. My younger sister had been banished a few years ago to some boarding school – I was too scared to ask where, or if I could see her. Only later did I find out that my sister had been unceremoniously dumped at an orphanage after being told that it was a boarding school.

Only my friend at the office knew something of the truth. But I was going to be losing her. She and her husband were emigrating to Canada to start a new life. She wanted me to go with them, but I couldn't even begin to fathom how that could work.

A few months later, after many letters back and forth, my friends sent me a plane ticket for a journey in three months' time. I couldn't believe it. I couldn't imagine using the ticket. I couldn't imagine NOT using it!

Finally, a week before the departure date, I told my mother that I was leaving. She laughed it off, saying that I was too stupid and weak to survive on my own in London. I then told her that I wasn't going to London, I was going to Canada, and I showed her the ticket. Then began the wind-up to a full-throttle beating. I knew the signs. First she would close all the windows so the neighbors couldn't hear. Then she would start the litany of verbal abuse and accusations, first in a whisper, then louder and louder until the shouts and the physical poundings reduced me to a whimper.

It was the last time she hit me.

I left England scarred, frightened, and alone, not understanding where the courage had come from to leave. Still hearing the mantra – 'You're stupid and useless, you'll never survive' – in my head, over and over again.

That fear and those feelings never left, until that moment, ten years later in the psychiatrist's office.

"Georgina, you do have choices."

"How can I help how I feel about my mother? How can I stop getting the shakes and shingles every time I get a letter from her?"

"What does the letter say?"

"I don't know … I didn't open it." I handed it over. He opened it and read it out loud.

> *Dear Gina:*
>
> *You are an ungrateful daughter. After everything I have done for you, this is how you treat me. You go to another country, get a good job, and don't care how I am. One letter a week is no way to treat your mother.*
>
> *You have no pride in who you are, just like your father; you are stupid and self centered. I worked hard all my life to feed and clothe you; this is the thanks I get. You wait until you have children of your own, then you'll understand.*
>
> *Your mother*

By the time he finished that letter – just like all the other letters she sent, I was sobbing and feeling small, alone, and ashamed that he could see the truth of me.

"This letter," he said, "makes me very angry. How does it make you feel?"

"Frightened and alone."

It was then he used the word CHOICE. "Georgina, your mother is in another country, and you have lived in another place for the ten years you have been here. Do you not make new choices every day for yourself? Didn't you choose your new apartment? Your job? Your clothes?"

"Yes, but I'm always frightened that I'm going to make the wrong choices, because I know I'm not smart."

"How else can you learn if you don't make mistakes? If you don't buy clothes you won't wear, or choose friends who aren't good for you, how will you learn to make the right choices?"

He had said this, or words like this, many times before. But this time it connected.

The light came on. I suddenly realized what he meant. I realized that even not making a choice, or doing what my mother wanted me to do, was a choice. So like it or not ... I WAS making choices.

What freedom! What joy! I started to laugh, and laugh, and laugh. Tears of laughter ran down my face. He sat and smiled and watched. "That's better. Much better. Now go home, and come back next week. I think you are ready to graduate to just once a week. Don't you?"

I was breathless with laughter, and giggles kept bubbling up from my stomach all the way home on the bus. What a revelation. I choose anyway ... I might as well get to make the choice I want! Wow!

Walking into my flat, I turned on the radio ... and chose a new radio station. My first real, proactive choice since I'd arrived ten years ago.

Starting small. But starting to choose.

~Dr. Georgina Cannon

These Things Shall Never Die

The pure, the bright, the beautiful, that stirred our
    hearts in youth,
The impulses to wordless prayer, the dreams of love
    and truth;
The longing after something's lost, the spirit's
    yearning cry,
The striving after better hopes – these things can
    never die.

The timid hand stretched forth, to aid a brother in
    his need,
A kindly word in grief's dark hour that proves a
    friend indeed:
The plea for mercy softly breathed, when justice
    threatens nigh,
The sorrow of a contrite heart – these things shall
    never die.

Let nothing pass, for every hand must find some
    work to do;
Lose not a chance to waken love – be firm, and just,
    and true:
So shall a light that cannot fade, beam on thee from
    on high.
And angel voices say to thee – these things shall
    never die.

~ Charles Dickens

Journey Back to Life

Whatever the tasks that your soul has agreed to, whatever
its contract with the Universe is, all of the experiences of
your life serve to awaken within you the memory of that
contract, and to prepare you to fulfill it.
— Gary Zukav

'This wasn't supposed to happen to me,' I thought as I sat
there, reeling with the news that I had HIV! I was a normal
twenty-nine-year-old, middle-class, Jewish girl from New York
– not promiscuous or gay, not an IV drug user.

My boyfriend and I had been dating for ten months when
the topic of my going back on birth control pills came up, so
I'd made an appointment at a local clinic. While there, I
requested a complete check-up. When asked if I wanted to
take the HIV test, I answered, "Sure, no problem." The counselor smiled during my pretest counseling. I signed the
papers, took the test, and was on my way. I was to return in
two weeks for my results. When I did, the counselor was no
longer smiling. In fact, she barely looked me in the face.

"I'm sorry," she said, "but your HIV test came back
positive."

"What!" I shouted, "No, no, no, this is a mistake. You
must have mixed up the blood samples!"

I sat there waiting for an answer that would make this
nightmare go away. She coldly said, "No, that does
not happen. We conducted two tests, the ELISA and the

Western Blot, and they both came back positive." That's all I heard.

I was going to die, and I was terrified. A hundred questions started racing through my mind. What is HIV? What will it do to my body? How can I tell my family? My boyfriend? How do I tell my mother that I may die before her? Am I going to be able to continue working my career as a caterer? Can I ever get married? Will I ever have children? Will anyone want to touch me or be intimate with me ever again? Who did this to me? Does my boyfriend have it too? Will he leave me? How long will I live? Will people be able to tell I have it, like a red dot on my forehead? I felt uneducated and ignorant. I wanted to scream, cry, run, hit a wall.

Once outside, I sat in my car, crying uncontrollably, unable to drive. I watched as an elderly woman crossed the street, extremely slowly. I was admiring her perseverance and independence and thought, *'I'm sure she has a lot of health challenges and adversities, but she's still plugging away.'* When she finally reached the other side, she became my inspiration. I thought, if she can do it, I can too. I don't remember driving home.

Once there, I immediately called my sister, needing to confide in her about my devastating diagnosis. I told her I was going to die. I also called my stepbrother and boyfriend. When I called my boyfriend and told him of my diagnosis, he said, "Don't worry, baby, I am there for you. I will be right over." Within two hours, they were at my house. I don't know how I would have handled this disastrous news without the love and support that surrounded me immediately.

We all sat in denial that evening, deciding I needed to be retested. But although I was retested three times, each time the results were positive. It was confirmed: I really had HIV.

It was extremely difficult to disclose what I was dealing with, without crying for the first year. I told my stepbrother to tell his mom, who told my dad, who told my mother. My immediate family continued to support me and continued to love me unconditionally. It took others time to accept that I was not a "bad girl." Because of ignorance, some of my important relationships changed course from that day forward.

Once I'd fully accepted that I was in fact HIV positive, I swung into action. I became a human sponge, learning everything I could about the disease and what it would do to my body. I learned that I would have to take steps to strengthen my immune system. That was the most important fact that would allow me to stay alive. What a mission for a twenty-nine-year-old!

I began living in a state of urgency. When I sought out support geared to heterosexuals, I discovered there was none. All I wanted was another female to identify with, to help me accept and understand what I was to face. Only one doctor's office offered a women's support group for HIV sufferers, but I soon discovered there were only two of us in attendance. 'Where is everyone?' I asked myself. I couldn't be the only one.

Four months after my diagnosis, my girlfriend invited me to join her on a trip to Greece and Italy for the summer. "Why not," I said, "I'm dying – let it be my last hurrah!"

Once there, I didn't want to return to my life, where I would have to face the reality of the disease I had. Material possessions no longer meant anything to me. But I knew I would eventually have to return and face the reality of a new and different life. When I finally returned to the USA, I left my apartment in Miami and went to New York City for the next six months, sleeping on various friends' couches and living out of a suitcase. When my credit cards were at their limit, my sister convinced me to come back to Miami in exchange for buying me the precious vitamins I needed to keep up my immune system.

I discovered to my relief that the women's HIV support group had grown to eight women. I decided to use my energy for something positive, so I began promoting the group in local clinics and libraries through flyers. I used my background in catering to get pastries donated to the group.

We called our support group "The Breakfast Club." I took it upon myself to bring resources and literature to the group each week and to peer counsel the other women, especially the newly diagnosed. To my delight, I discovered I was a natural therapist and that I had a purpose!

I threw a party August 11, 1995 at a local HIV/AIDS agency to bring the straight men out of hiding. I wanted to meet someone, since the men in the doctor's offices weren't looking at me. Dating is hard enough without having a contagious disease.

Soon after the party, an AIDS agency asked me to become involved on a Ryan White Council. In exchange, I asked to use their lounge area to have a party. Again I drew on my catering background to plan the event by getting food donated and flyers designed. The agency gave me a list of fax numbers and access to their fax.

To my delight, twenty-five people showed up to that first party! There was a great deal of laughter as people shared their disclosure stories, talked for the first time with others who had the same concerns, and shared T-cell counts and vitamin regimens. Many said they had not talked to anyone besides their own doctor in five years. They could finally talk without fear, and their feelings of isolation were relieved. Phone numbers were being exchanged, and people were laughing! It was a wonderful beginning. Word began to spread about what I was doing so that month after month, more and more people showed up.

That's how Positive Connections, our support center, was born. Since then, it has grown from a 500-square-foot office, to 2,000 square feet, to a 3,500-square-foot office nine years later, with nine employees and a $400,000 annual budget! Since we opened, we have provided services and programs to over 1,500 HIV-positive individuals. Each year we provide dinner lectures, holistic services, support groups, mental health therapy, health fairs, peer counseling, social activities, annual parties, a speaker's bureau, a newsletter, a web site, a lending library, and a resource center.

While it is true that I have been jokingly dubbed a 'yenta,'* I take special pride in the fact that The Center for Positive Connections (TCPC) has been responsible for the development of hundreds of "positive" friendships, relationships, connections, and dozens of marriages – PROOF "positive" that life after an HIV diagnosis is possible.

We opened another office in New York City three years ago, with a monthly support group and bi-monthly social gatherings. My goal is to expand and offer my integrated holistic model in all major cities in the US.

Today I still travel around the country teaching others to follow my model. I never thought my resume would list so many accomplishments, nor did I ever dream that one day I'd be in *People* magazine or on the Montel Williams Show. Seventeen years have passed since I was first diagnosed with HIV, and to this day I continue to live without medications.

It was when I thought I would die that I really started to live. Having HIV has been a gift that has turned my life from one of searching for a purpose to living that purpose every day.

~ *Sheri Kaplan*

yenta: a person regarded as meddlesome.

Crossing Over

I wanted a perfect ending. Now I've learned, the hard way,
that some poems don't rhyme, and some stories don't have
a clear beginning, middle, and end. Life is about not
knowing, having to change, taking the moment and making
the best of it, without knowing what's going to happen next.
Delicious ambiguity.

– Gilda Radner

The Emperor's New Clothes

If the soul's light had to stay inside its house
I'd open every door and window!
~ Rumi

A human life has seasons, much as the earth has seasons, each time with its own particular beauty and power. And gifts. By focusing on springtime and summer, we have turned the natural process of life into a process of loss rather than a process of celebration and appreciation. Life is neither linear nor is it stagnant. It is movement from mystery to mystery. Just as a year includes autumn and winter, life includes death, not as an opposite, but as an integral part of the way life is made.

The denial of death is the most common way we all edit life. Despite the power of technology to reveal to us the nature of the world, death remains the ultimate unknown, impervious to the prodding finger of science. We might well ask if anything which cannot be addressed in scientific terms is really worthy of our attention. Yet most of the things that give life its depth, meaning, and value are impervious to science.

In 1974 I became interested in working with people facing death. I had thought to study death itself much as I had studied any other new field that had attracted my professional interest. I began in our library with a search of the current literature. This library serves a major medical school and hospital, and it is one of the largest and best medical libraries in the United States. Approaching a librarian, I asked if she could direct me to the periodicals on death. "Do you mean *Cancer Research* and the *Journal of Oncology?*" she responded, "Or the *American Journal of Cardiology?*" We stared at each other for a moment. "Death," I said.

Confused, she lowered her eyes and began to search her index under "D," finally coming up with a location deep in the library stacks. Following her instructions, I went downstairs past floors and floors of medical journals and books to the right floor. There, searching through rows of ceiling to floor shelves filled with journals and periodicals, I found the section on death at last. It was a single shelf, almost empty, which contained five outdated issues of *Journal of Thanatology,* two books on the pastoral counseling of the bereaved, and a copy of the New Testament.

After the initial shock, I remember thinking that I must be face-to-face with the Shadow of contemporary medicine. Surely the hundreds of thousands of journals and books I had just passed to get here might be thought of as a massive response to the possibility of death. Yet death itself was hidden, barely given shelf space in this vast body of knowledge that represented the state of the art of medicine. At that time, every medical school in the United States was set up in the very same way. Many still are.

At the time of my brush with death in the medical stacks, death occupied the same position in my consciousness that it occupied in the medical library. In fact, the medical library might have been an externalization of my own mind. As is true for most doctors, I had been present at a death only when my frantic efforts to prevent it had failed. I put these deaths behind me as quickly as I could and filled my mind with the countless facts about disease and cure on which my skills were based.

My first experience of death as something other than professional failure occurred when I was director of the pediatric inpatient division of Mount Zion Hospital, an inner-city hospital in San Francisco. I had not known then that death can be a time of healing, or that sometimes, shortly before people die, their wholeness can be directly experienced by others.

Arriving for work one morning, I was alarmed to hear angry voices coming through my closed office door. Inside, several of the staff nurses and resident doctors were arguing in an uncharacteristically emotional scene. The subject of this angry interchange was one of the patients, a five-year-old boy who was in the end stages of leukemia. Apparently this morning the child had told the nurse who awakened him that he was going home today. "Help me pack my things," he demanded, pointing with excitement to his tiny suitcase in the closet.

The nurse was horrified. Who could have promised this terribly sick little boy that he could go home when he had no platelets or white cells? When everyone knew he was so fragile he could bleed to death from the slightest injury? She asked the other nurses on her shift and the previous shift if they had told the child he might go home. No one had said a word to him.

The outraged nurses then accused the young doctors. The doctors were incensed at the suggestion that it was one of them who had callously promised such an impossible thing. The discussion had grown more heated then and was moved to the privacy of my office. "Could he go home by ambulance, just for an hour?" they asked me, unwilling to disappoint him and destroy his hopes. It seemed too dangerous.

"Did anybody ask him who told him he could go home?" I said. Of course, no one had wanted to talk to him about that. I felt suddenly tired, but I said, "I'll go and talk to him."

He was sitting on his bed pillow, facing the door, and coloring in a book when I entered the room. I was struck by how emaciated, how sickly he was. He looked up from his coloring and our eyes met. In that moment things changed.

The room became very still, and there seemed to be a sort of yellowish cast to the light. I had a sense of an enormous presence, and I remember thinking wildly that we had stepped outside of time. Suddenly I was aware of the overwhelming guilt I felt about this little boy. For months I had done things to him that caused him pain, and I still had not been able to cure him. I had avoided him then and felt ashamed. As our eyes met, it seemed that somehow he understood this and forgave me. All at once I was able to forgive myself, not just for this little boy, but for all the children I had treated and hurt and couldn't help throughout my career. It was a sort of healing.

His frailty and my tiredness fell away, and we seemed to recognize each other. In that moment we became equals, two souls who had played out our difficult roles in a drama with absolute impeccability, he as a little boy and I as a doctor. The drama was complete. I had served some unknown purpose, and there was nothing to forgive or be forgiven. There was just a deep sense of acceptance and mutual respect. All this happened in a heartbeat.

Then he spoke to me. In a voice filled with joy, he said, "Dr. Remen, I'm going home." By now I was speechless. I mumbled something like, "I'm so glad," and I backed out, closing the door behind me.

I returned to my office very confused and shaken by the experience. "What did he say?" the staff demanded. I told them that I hadn't asked. "Why don't we just wait a little while and see what happens?" A few hours later, the child said he was tired. He lay down, pulling his sheet over his head, and quietly slipped away.

The staff took his death hard. He was a love of a little boy, and they had cared for him for a long time. Yet many told me privately how relieved they were that he had died before he discovered that someone had lied to him, and he couldn't go home.

Perception may require a certain openness. We see what

our lives have made us ready to see. This child had known that he was going home in a much more profound sense than the staff was prepared to appreciate. At that time I had no way to make sense of this experience either, so I did the comfortable thing: I forgot it.

About a year after my trip to the library to study death, I began to have a series of vivid, disturbing dreams. I would find myself once again at the bedside of pediatric patients who had died many years before. Before I went to sleep, I would not have been able to remember these children's names, but in the dreams I would again know all of their lab values, be able to recall the pictures on their bedside tables, the names of their beloved stuffed animals, and even the pattern of their nightshirts. Unbidden, I would see clearly the many things that I had not fully seen when I had actually been there. I would hear again whole conversations, word for word, conversations filled with hope and fear, loss and love. I would see every nuance of expression on the faces of people whom I had not thought about in years. It was as if I had saved somewhere the experiences I had refused to live before. But the most frightening thing about these dreams was that eventually in each one I would come to feel what I had not allowed myself to feel: feelings of sadness, pain, helplessness, and loss. I would awaken sobbing uncontrollably, sometimes for hours.

These dreams occurred nightly. After four or five of them, I called a friend who was a psychiatrist and poured out my concern and fright. I was afraid to go to sleep. Was I going crazy? "I don't think so," he said, and asked me if I felt willing to stay with it to see what it might mean. I was not sure that I could. "You can call me every morning and tell me about your dream," he offered. And so I did.

In the end I had twenty or more of these dreams. And gradually something changed. I began to know how much I had cared about these children, how meaningful and irreplaceable their lives had been, and to wonder if their deaths had any meaning also. Eventually I began to experience the great emptiness left by their passing, and at last I was able to genuinely wonder where they had gone. In the end I, who had taken death so personally, no longer saw it as a personal failure but as a universal mystery. I began to remember older experiences, experiences from my childhood, times before death was the enemy. I also remembered the little boy who told me he was going home. Something inside me that had closed its eyes and run from death for years had turned again and wanted to see. To be there. As a preparation for my work with people who were facing life-threatening illness and possible death, these dreams turned out to be far more important than the expertise I had hoped to find in the library.

~Rachel Naomi Remen, M. D.

Grappling With Destiny

Every creature is a word of God.
– Meister Eckhart

As any of you who have recurrent cancer know, the experience changes. I am sure that people on their first round know that, too. It is very much an up-and-down ride into despair and back into hope again. At the beginning I did conventional and unconventional treatments. My idea was that the more I did, the more chance I would have never to have to face the beast again.

So I did everything I could find. I did the conventional treatments, surgery, and chemotherapy. I did acupuncture, herbs, diet, and a whole lot of soul searching. And bottom line, this has been a spiritual journey for me. I think that is what is hardest to talk about because it's the most numinous, but it is also the important part of this experience for me.

I find that when I am in periods of rest, in-between facing the cancer moving in my body, I think I have found answers. I think that I can look at my experiences and say, "Oh yes, I did this and this right, and therefore I am here." And then it comes back and I think, "Well, maybe I didn't do this and this right." What I find is that facing cancer as it returns brings up questions. And the questions are deepening questions for me, and that is why it's a spiritual journey.

To give you a little perspective on me, before I had cancer, I was what I call a human doing. I was trying to be a recovering human doing, but failing. I thrived on being busy all the time, and I did really well with solving problems by using my mental abilities. We are all trained to do this well in our culture. In a sense you can think of that as the masculine expression – the rational, the expressive, the doing. I was good at relying on that in my life, and it had done well for me.

But I found when I got cancer that this expression didn't work for me as well anymore. I went to many experts, got many points of view, and found that none of them agreed. I couldn't find treatment decisions that added up and made total sense to me. I was left to make decisions from some different place.

What I found was that some treatments work for some people – all treatments work for some people. No treatments work for everyone, and I could find experts who would defend to their death each different treatment for me.

I realized I had to find a new place in myself from which to make my decisions, and that is what has taken me in deeper. I have also given myself permission during my healing time to go off-line, to stop my doing, and just be quiet. I have discovered the real beauty of having quiet time. Just time for hangin' out.

In 1992, the first time that the cancer recurred, it came back to my liver. The doctors to whom I was going to complain about the symptoms I was having, kind of kept soothing me and saying, "It's just your nerves, these feelings you're having in your solar plexus." When the cancer was finally diagnosed, it had taken over 80% of my liver. One doctor that I went to said, "If you don't start chemotherapy within ten days, it will be too late, and you will be dead within two months from liver failure."

Well, that got my attention. I had been really determined not to do anything toxic to my body again, but everyone to whom I spoke (and I spoke to a lot of non-conventional therapists with nontoxic alternatives), said, "Your liver is too far gone for our treatments to work for you." So I was called to stretch my acceptance of God's work to include, once again, chemotherapy.

I had always been Ms. Natural and never even took aspirin. I had natural childbirth, the whole thing. I ate a vegetarian diet – I had been on the "cancer" diet for 25 years. I told myself, *God works through human beings, and the intention of chemotherapy is to heal. It is not my choice of method, but I will know when I need to stop it – my doctor won't.*

The whole process for me has been a series of decisions to take charge of my life as I take charge of my treatments, realizing that while doctors are my consultants, I am the one expert about myself. So I go for information to the doctors, and then I go to my quiet place inside me, and I find the answer that brings me peace at that time. For that moment it was chemotherapy.

During the winter of 1992, I came very close to dying. By Thanksgiving, most of my medical professionals, which included an oncologist, a Chinese medical doctor, an acupuncturist, an herbalist, and all kinds of support, were saying quietly behind my back that I would not make it until Christmas. Well, I did make it until Christmas – and then I got sicker.

I would like to share a little bit about that experience because I want to emphasize once again that this experience of having cancer is very unique. *Everyone's journey is their own.* So something that works for me doesn't necessarily work for anyone else, and vice versa.

I just want to encourage you, as you listen to other people's healing stories, listen with your heart, and listen with openness, but don't listen for answers for yourself. It is the process that you want to hear. I think that healing is a process of involvement, of acceptance, and of going ahead – whatever that takes.

Anyway, before I got really sick, my friends assigned me the job to just breathe. They said, "That is all you need to do.

You don't need to be doing things all the time. In your recovery, the mantra you need to repeat is, Just Breathe."

Well, that winter I got really sick. I was on IV nutrition because I couldn't eat. I lost so much weight that I looked like a starvation victim, except my belly looked like I was nine months pregnant with twins. I got very, very weak. I called myself "the houseplant." People would feed me, move me into places in the sun, and generally take care of me. "Just breathe" was about what I could do, and even that was hard because my lungs were filling with fluid.

I remember one day sitting out on the deck, watching the leaves moving on the trees and thinking, *Do I want to fight my way back?* I was in what I called the void. I think we often go through a deep valley when facing possible death. For me it was a spiritual crisis. I had always believed that life continues after death, and I had been called to see if this was a head belief or a core belief.

What I found was, as I hung out in that deep, quiet place, just breathing, that I felt two things. One thing was that God, Great Spirit, Life, whatever you want to call it, did not care if I had skin on or not. That the reality of my life would go on if I was in this body or not. I wondered then, 'Who chooses? Do I get to choose if I live, or is that the will of something greater than I am?' I never got an answer to that one; I am still working that one out.

But I really got to a place where, aside from a tug of sadness about leaving my loved ones, I could see that both choices were viable. I could either live in my body, or I could go on living without my body. Either way was okay. So there I was, sitting out on the deck on that day and feeling the pain of human life, feeling the pain of the world, and feeling totally overwhelmed by it. I had always felt that the world needed fixing and that I needed to fix it, so I was really overwhelmed. At that moment, I thought, *I don't think so. I don't think that I do want to fight my way back. It is just too painful out there. I think I will just let go, and go on.*

I had this thought, I won't call it a voice – it was a thought that popped into my mind that said, *You don't need to do anything. You just need to be an entry point for love – that's all.* And I realized, sitting on my deck chair wrapped in blankets, just breathing, that I could do that even there. I didn't have to do anything more than just open to love and let it pour through me. It would benefit the people around me and who knows, it might ripple out, across the world. There are spiritual traditions that say that the flutter of a butterfly's wings on this continent can affect the weather in China. Certainly if I aligned myself with love, it would make a difference.

With that realization I thought, *Okay, I could come back.* I began to get better, though I reached a point where I decided not to do any more chemotherapy. I wanted to do something that had more hope, and chemo didn't offer a whole lot of long-term hope for someone in my situation.

My husband found a clinical trial using monoclonal antibodies. When we called to see if they could take me, they were just starting their next round. The timing was perfect. What I learned from that again is that I am the one who knows when I can start treatment, when I can stop treatment, and what treatment to take. I just need to have people who can consult with me along the way to give me the information I need for that.

I got on the clinical trial. It was a non-toxic biological trial. It was one of these incredible things where they genetically engineer antibodies, then infuse them in your body. The antibodies go in and tie up the cancer cells. For sixteen months I improved. I got better, stronger. I got back to nearly total health. And then for some unknown reason in August, the cancer started to progress again.

One person I know says cancer does that. It has quiet times, and then it has active times. My tendency is to say, "What was I doing wrong? What can I change?" Because naturally I want to control it, so if I can figure out something I can do that will affect it, then I will do it.

What I am doing as I grapple with my relationship to my destiny is that I am finding nontoxic treatments. I am doing shark cartilage right now. I am looking for other kinds of things that I can do to support my immune system. I'm working a lot with prayer. I find that my appreciation for the mystery of life has grown so much since I have been on this journey. I find it hard to pray for healing, because we have such a small part of the picture that we can see. We never know when our experience can be helping others that we love, or those who are around us.

Anytime that I pray for my healing I add, "But not my will, this or something better." And I pray for the strength, the courage, and the clarity to align with God's will for me. Whatever that is, wherever that takes me. I find that what is important to me as I go through life now, is strengthening my attunement to that place in me that is hooked up to the universe. That place in me that knows, that place in me that is quiet and wise, that can go into the darkness and hold the questions and not fall apart at not having the answers.

As I live with that, I realize that I am preparing just as well for death, whenever that happens, as I am for life. I think, bottom line, that is what everyone needs to be doing. If all of us, in our whole culture, not just people who are sick, lived our lives as though we were preparing for death, I think our lives would be much richer and more whole. I think our world would be a better place.

One final thought – I think that cancer is in part sort of a karmic thing that humanity has generated. People with cancer have been volunteered; we are the mine canaries, who show that this is a toxic environment that we are living in. Not just toxic chemically, but toxic emotionally and psychologically. I feel that as we learn to heal ourselves, as we learn to go into the unknown, as we learn to go into the silence and create spaces for that silence, as we learn to align with the goddess – as we go into the parts of our being that our culture has forgotten, we will not only be healing ourselves and our lives, but we will be helping to heal our society.

~Merrily Bronson

My Last Journey

How do I make my last journey?
How will I mark this path I've trod?
When I, forever Soul, move on
Will there be a print in sod?

I've taken in lifetimes of knowledge,
Inner journeys allow me to see
That there is only one Great Truth:
In God's love I will always be.

Yet knowledge is a feeble thing
When met with wisdom beyond time.
All earthly beings must expire,
Every reason must have rhyme.

How can I take my last journey?
My aching footsteps fail me,
And I ask you for the Strength to trust.
I don't know how to leave this life.
I only know I must.

~Ruth Edgett

Why I Lived, And Why I Died

Because I could not stop for death, He kindly
stopped for me;
The carriage held but just ourselves and immortality.
– Emily Dickinson

It was the Labour Day weekend, and we were together at our stepsister's home in New Brunswick, Canada, grieving the loss of my father rather than enjoying the family picnic we had planned. Our dad, a diabetic, had died suddenly during the night due to complications of an operation to amputate a portion of his infected foot. The stress on his body had caused a heart attack.

The suddenness of his passing, and the fact that none of us were with him when he died, caused me the deepest sadness imaginable. Peter, the priest in the family, tried to reassure us all that indeed Dad had not been alone when he died, but that he was safe in the arms of God.

My mom, who had been divorced from Dad for years, lived with Cathy in Hamilton, Ontario. A week had passed since the picnic when I got a desperate call from Cathy. She had noticed that Mom's face appeared yellow, and she was very concerned.

The diagnosis was pancreatic cancer, and surgery was scheduled to bypass the blocked bile duct. I was shocked when we were told that Mom's time with us was short.

Nine months later, our youngest sister Maureen flew in from New Brunswick to be at Mom's bedside. We all realized there was no hope of her coming home from the hospital this time, and we three sisters had sworn that Mom would not be alone at any time during her final days and hours.

Mom spoke for the last time on Friday night when she said her last goodbyes. On Sunday afternoon, the three of us held vigil as her breathing slowed. Mom's sisters and our uncle were present as well. We laughed at the stories our aunts told about Mom's antics over the years. As Mom slipped away, Cathy and Maureen sobbed in each other's arms behind the half-drawn hospital curtain. I held Mom's hand and told her to go to her mom, to Grandma, and then in a scene that emblazoned itself on my mind, she took a final, agonizing breath. I remember thinking that the movies sure have it wrong. The gentle release I'd envisioned for Mom hadn't been peaceful at all. I realized that dying, like being born, could be hard work.

My legs felt stiff and wobbly as we three sisters held each other as we walked down the hospital corridor to a room provided for us to grieve.

All of a sudden I felt a presence of divine comfort and calmness surround me. Before I could tell the others what I was experiencing, Maureen said, "It's Mom; she's doing something ... I feel better!"

"Me too!" I said. It was like Mom was infusing each of us with her love.

Next Maureen saw Mom there in spirit, looking beautiful and healthy. She described to us how in her vision she saw Mom being reunited with her baby sister Frannie, who had died many years before at age three. Frannie was more like a daughter than a sister to her, and Mom never got over not being present when sweet Frannie, a Down's syndrome child, died suddenly. Now, in Maureen's vision, Mom and Frannie danced together joyfully in a kind of ring-around-the rosey as Mom sang with joy, "I know why I lived! I know why I died!"

Maureen's vision helped to heal much of the sadness we felt over Mom's prolonged illness and difficult passing. Even more, it helped to heal the regret we felt over our absence at the moment of Dad's death.

Two days later we were driving to the funeral home in a Toronto neighborhood. Mom's wake, funeral, and final resting place would be the same as her mother's.

"This is the right street, but where is it?" We each strained our necks looking out the car windows to find the building.

We all saw it at the same time – a rainbow across the sky coming through the roof of the funeral home! What startled us the most was that it hadn't even rained. We all laughed together at the amazing coincidence.

"Thanks, Mom!" we all chimed in unison.

I know now that Father Peter was right. Dad hadn't been alone when he died. None of us ever is. Thanks to the journey my parents started me on, I don't have to wait to begin to understand why I lived or why I will die, for I now realize that birth and death are an illusion. Life goes on beyond this form.

Thank you, Mom and Dad. I'll be seeing you.

~ Judy Prang

A Taste of Death

Courage is the price that Life exacts for granting peace.
The soul that knows it not, knows no release from little
things: Knows not the livid loneliness of fear, nor the mountain heights where bitter joy can hear the sound of wings.
— Amelia Earhart

We'd been at a day-long planning meeting in another city.
During the two-hour drive home, I slowly began to feel ill.
"Perhaps you're just hungry," my always-caring husband
suggested. We stopped at a roadside restaurant to test out his
theory and also feed the ever-hungry, reed-thin friend who'd
hitched a ride home with us.

I was incredibly dizzy as we entered the restaurant, and
my stomach was beginning to roll. Ever the stoic, I ordered
what I thought to be the least offensive food: a bowl of vanilla
ice cream. I ate a few spoonfuls and then 'played' with the
rest while I waited for my husband and our mutual friend to
finish their meals. Back in the car, my head pounded without
mercy.

When we finally arrived home after dropping our friend
off, I made what seemed to be an eternal trek from the car to
the living room sofa. I remained there, except for trips to the
bathroom, for four days. Never having made it to a doctor, I
could only surmise that I had a bad case of food poisoning.

On the evening of the fourth day, I desperately needed a
change of scenery, so I slowly made my way to our upstairs

bedroom. Weak and sweating and trembling uncontrollably from the effort, I half crawled, half fell onto the bed.

I dreamt of Native Americans coming through the walls of my room and of a shaman who chanted and waved medicine bags over my fevered body. It was a very potent dream, calling up memories of a race to which I once belonged. When I awoke, although still weak from days of no food and little water, I felt considerably better.

A strange sound coming from one corner of the room drew my attention. I shifted positions for a better look, hardly expecting to see what I saw: a floor-to-ceiling swirling light so bright as to cause a sharp pain in my eyes. The sound became a howling wind.

Was I awake – I'd thought so – or was this yet another dream? I closed and re-opened my eyes several times, testing the vision. The light never went away. It was as real as the bedroom itself.

A voice invited me to enter the vortex of light and sound. "You have come to a place where you can choose to stay on earth or leave," it said with loving indifference.

Leaving my body behind on the bed, I cautiously moved into the whirlpool. The deeper in I went, the more mellow the light and sound became. A sense of well-being washed over me.

Without the entrapments of the mind and body, death, I observed, was actually a very pleasant experience. There was no fear, no heart-wrenching sadness at leaving my beloved Jerry behind, no concerns about any unfinished business … it was a pure and gentle experience.

"No," I shouted suddenly. My voice reverberated down the endless corridor. "I choose to stay on earth. There is so much more to learn, and to give. I choose to stay." There was a loud swooshing sound and the sense of incredible speed as I returned to the body on the bed.

The doorway of light closed behind me. The room was

now engulfed in the stillness of earth's twilight. I eased into a healing night's sleep.

Illness-induced illusion? Reality? It doesn't matter – the result was the same. I now live life without the fear of my inevitable crossover. I have tasted death and found the experience itself to be very, very sweet. I look forward to tasting it again – when the time is right.

~ Jo Leonard

Contemplation on Monet's Water Lilies

The light on the water is like white fire,
Dancing up in little peaks,
Twirling under and around
The petals and the leaves.

In this vision
Fire and water become one,
And if you gaze softly,
You will hear music,
First faintly and then more clear,
Delicate notes floating
Like petals on water,
Melody liquid and rich.

And if your eye follows the fire,
It becomes a road stretching out in the distance,
The lilies become clouds
Suspended on the horizon,
And the brilliance draws you on.

~ Laura Reave

On Finding Purpose

At the center of the Universe is a loving heart that
continues to beat and that wants the best for every person.
Anything that we can do to help foster the intellect and
spirit and emotional growth of our fellow human beings,
that is our job. Those of us who have this particular vision
must continue against all odds. Life is for service.

–Fred Rogers
(a.k.a., "Mister Rogers"), 1928-2003

A Prayer to Know One's Calling

Often times when I'm speaking publicly or getting together with listeners, I am asked if I always knew that I wanted to be in radio. The answer is not a simple one, but I swear to you it's the truth. You couldn't make this up.

I was in my final year of high school, and it was April. By now most of my friends had already decided on their schools and career paths. But not me! I had toyed with the idea of teaching, but dreaded sitting behind a desk. I knew that my place was in front of people, but I couldn't possibly be tied down to a 9 to 5 job. I was getting frustrated and not just a little panicked at the thought that I hadn't yet heard my calling.

My mother was a registered nurse. I could never follow in her squishy footsteps; I hate the sight of blood and don't have the unique blend of compassion and sangfroid required to be a good nurse. My dad was a pilot in the Air Force, then for commercial airlines. His advice to his four daughters: "Find a good rut and get comfortable; you're in it a long time." Imagine that! A career sounded more like a life sentence than an adventure. Was this to be my future too?

The day that I began to learn the answer to that question is as clear in my mind as if it happened to me yesterday.

It was early on a chilly spring morning; I was tearing out of my bedroom (late as usual) to catch the bus that would take me on the forty-five minute ride to high school. It was a special day: all of the seniors were to gather at school, then board a bus that would take us to another school where we would hear about courses and jobs that were available to us.

But as I stumbled through my bedroom, pulling on my green uniform vest as I went, I stopped and looked at my dark cork bulletin board. Pinned to it was "A Prayer to Know One's Calling." It had been handed out by a teacher months earlier, and I'd never even looked at the little card. But that morning I paused and read it over, taking in the words, which I believe were similar to these:

Jesus, Divine Caller of vocations,
You invite some to chosen professions,
Others to distinctive spiritual work!
Your call may reflect one's ambitions,
Or may be a command to a special calling.
Inspire me to always know within my heart
What particular type of work is fitting
To do Your will at that particular time.
Your many callings vary immensely.
They are all reflections of Your Holiness.
Thank you for my heavenly calling and
For maintaining the vocation of Your choice!

Despite stopping to read the card, I still managed to catch the short yellow bus that waited outside for me. But because our connecting bus was delayed, ours was the last group of students to arrive at the Career Day gathering. I had to squeeze my name onto the bottom of a couple of sign-up sheets. I remember that one speaker was to share his experiences as a recently released prisoner. The other speaker, I don't recall. But it didn't matter – by the time I signed up, they were both fully booked anyway.

Disappointed and wondering why I was wasting my time, I plunked myself down at a desk in a strange classroom. Soon I found myself listening to a professor from the local community college, Loyalist in Belleville, talking about its two-year radio course. As this colorful, funny, corny former radio announcer launched into his spiel, I sat up straight. So did the hair on the back of my neck. My skin began to tingle, I felt a rush of adrenalin, and I'm sure my heartbeat must have doubled, so excited was I about what I heard. Before that moment I was lost, unsure not only of what I wanted to do, but what I was meant to do.

Suddenly, like a flash of lightning, it had all become clear. I was soon to learn that the college had closed applications for that fall's course. However, I was allowed to audition and miraculously, a spot for me appeared. Two years later, I graduated Dean's List with a perfect 4.0 average (after having never even cracked the honor roll in high school). I started my first news job at Ottawa's number one station. I was on my way!

When I look back on that day, I wonder how I could possibly have been so blind to the myriad signs in my life that had been pointing me toward a career in radio. I'd always loved to read aloud in class; my favorite pastime as a child was taping "funny" interviews and Q & A's into a cassette recorder. I'd always felt comfortable in front of a microphone, having sung with my grandfather's small dance band in Alberta, and having done the morning announcements over my high school's PA system. I couldn't begin to count how many days I carried a transistor radio in my pocket to keep me company, or how many nights I fell asleep listening to compelling news magazines like CBC Radio's *As It Happens* (hosted by two women). My heart would race as I wondered how they had the nerve to ask all of those "important" people such tough questions. Some nights I could hardly get to sleep! But little did I know that their medium would become my own, and it would lead me to a life beyond my wildest dreams.

Not everything has been perfect. I've encountered plenty of obstacles, but I know that they've helped guarantee that my own career would never be described as a "rut." Most importantly, I have never once regretted choosing this path – or rather, accepting the one that was chosen for me.

Looking back on that day 25 years ago, I see now that the road to a career in radio was laid out ahead of me as surely as if God had folded a treasure map into a paper plane and sent it sailing toward me. I am so grateful that I finally quit ducking and let it hit me between the eyes. Sometimes that's what it takes – a cosmic smack upside the head – before we stop and take notice of what the universe is trying so hard to tell us. Maybe if I'd just heard it on the radio! So keep listening. You never know what you're really meant to hear.

~ *Erin Davis*

Opening My Eyes to the Light

If we don't change, we don't grow.
If we don't grow, we are not really living.
Growth demands a temporary surrender of security.
– Gail Sheehy

It was March break 1997, and my three-year-old son had just said goodbye to a little friend who had slept over the night before. At the age of thirty-five, I felt that my life was in complete harmony and balance as never before. My husband and I were doing well in our careers and finances, and my first and only child was a sweet, easy boy who was a pleasure to be with. The early years of my life had been tremendously challenging and unstable, and so with this peaceful, safe, and happy lifestyle, I felt had finally found security and stability.

It was dinner hour and since it was only March, the sun set quite quickly, and there was still a blanket of old winter snow on the ground. Rush hour had started, and my husband was in his usual place, slowly inching his way home on a crowded highway. He commuted to the office daily, and his travels usually took a couple of hours there and back.

My son Taylor was sitting in front of me watching TV in the living room while I began dinner activity in the kitchen. Innocence or ignorance, it's hard to say now, but I decided to make a simple meal for my very picky toddler. Putting a single egg into a plastic measuring cup with some water, I set it into the microwave and hit the start button. The egg was in the shell.

When the microwave dinged its completion, I drew the bubbling cup of water out. Automatically, I glanced into the cup as I started to set it on the counter. The next thing I can vividly recall is the sound of an explosion, loud enough that I thought someone had blown a tire right inside my living room, and then unimaginable pain, as I felt my eyes melt beneath my two hands, which were now cupping them in terror.

The pain was indescribable, but it was the fear and realization of what had just occurred that shot through my heart the most. I remember thinking to myself, "You've really done it this time." I knew the damage was bad, very bad. My face was on fire, and I could immediately feel my eyeballs swelling underneath my burning lids. I knew I was screaming and was pretty much hysterical, fumbling around and unable to see.

Quickly, my brain was scanning for a rational plan of action. I couldn't see the phone to dial it, my son was too small to trust to send outside for help, and I cringed at thinking about crawling in the dark and cold snow to cross the front yard to my neighbor's house. I didn't even know if they were home yet.

I yelled for Taylor to come to me, who was surprisingly very calm and quiet. I picked him up and told him that Mommy had hurt herself and couldn't see, so he was going to have to push the buttons 9-1-1 on the wall phone. We had talked about emergency and 911, but I had my doubts as to whether he could actually do it. After all, he was only three. What if he forgot his numbers from the pressure?

I felt him reach out and push buttons on the phone. I set him down and took the receiver from him. It was emergency services on the other end. My smart little boy had got it right. I became even more hysterical hearing someone else's voice. The dispatch woman was not impressed. She yelled back at me to quiet down and stop panicking. I wanted to reach through the phone line to strangle and shake her. "I'm blind, I'm burned, I have a right to be hysterical," I screamed back.

Despite my hysteria, and her impatience with me, I found myself hanging up with the reassurance that an ambulance was on its way. The fire hall was just around the corner, so I knew it wasn't going to take long.

Suddenly, I remembered my husband. This time I dialed his cell phone by counting the positions of the buttons on the phone from memory, as I had calmed down enough to focus. I succeeded and of course, began to cry. My poor husband couldn't make out a word, but he knew something was very wrong at home. I told my story the best I could, and said that the ambulance was already here and that I'd let him know what to do.

The paramedics came down the hall and they were men with angel-souls; my blindness made me know this more deeply. I felt their goodness coming towards me down the hall. Firemen and the police, and several neighbors I was told later accompanied the paramedics. My dear neighbors agreed to take care of Taylor, called Steve and re-routed him to the hospital, and cleaned up my kitchen. I was also told later that there was egg everywhere.

The paramedics had to lay me down and try to flush out my eyes of egg and eggshell. All the way to the hospital they joked and comforted me. They were amazing.

Once we reached the hospital, I was wheeled straight to the emergency room. My situation was critical. Most of the experience was a blur of noise and voices, but one voice in particular touched me the whole time: the voice of the attending nurse who stayed by my side holding my hand. This woman was gentle and kind, a magical mixture of humor and caring, another angel sent to me in my hour of darkness. To this day, I regret never having returned to the hospital to find her and thank her for her compassion to a terrified stranger whose life had changed forever in a flash.

My husband Steve arrived sometime during my emergency care; I can't recollect how we greeted each other for the first time not looking into each other's eyes. I knew my face was a mess; everyone's silence told me that loud and clear. Funny, how we bury deep our greatest pain when it becomes too big to face. I just didn't want to think about what all of this meant, not right then. All bandaged up like a war casualty; I was led home where Steve's parents waited, having arrived to put my son to bed. Thus began my long journey in blackness.

The pain was excruciating, and my swollen eyes oozed non-stop, so my bandages had to be changed often. I must have looked like an alien with my eye sockets swelled to the size of baseballs. I do remember asking someone to take a picture of me, but no one did. The next day Steve drove me to a doctor we were referred to. In his anxiety and stress to dress and ready both of us, he ended up at the doctor's office in his slippers. We had a good laugh about that when he discovered it.

The drive to the doctor's office was anguished. I remember turning my head to face my window in the car so I could cry without Steve noticing. It was the first time it struck me that I might never see again. The tears welled up inside my eyes, but couldn't find their way out, so they just burned inside my head, and I felt as if I would explode. There was no release, it seemed; I couldn't even shed my tears. When Steve took me out of the car, the noise of traffic passing by hit me first. I froze on the spot, thinking he had parked in the middle of the road, and I was going to be run over any minute. He reassured me that we were far from the road, safely parked in the parking lot. We shuffled along the icy path like a pair of seniors holding each other up. I suddenly had new respect for blind people who have the courage to walk about alone with just a cane to guide them. The world was quickly becoming a new place where I had no eyes to see.

When finally the doctor took me in, I braced myself for the worst. He removed my bandages and tried gently to pry my left eye open to look inside. I wanted to scream from the pain, but I bit my tongue. My eye was open, but I saw nothing.

'I'm blind,' I thought to myself, 'Just face it.' He told Steve it was too soon to tell anything right now and that we were to see him in a week. I think I tried to cry again on the way home.

I moved in for a week with Steve's parents. Taylor was with me, so Steve could continue to work. My dignity went out the window, as I had to be fed, bathed, led to the bathroom, and dressed by my mother-in-law. You end up going somewhere else in your mind so you can detach from what you must go through and not go insane. My in-laws were wonderful, infinitely patient, catering to me like a little child and looking after Taylor. I'm not sure how the days passed when I was just sitting around unseeing, unmoving, but they did.

The most painful moments were not when my bandages were changed, but when my little boy spoke to me. It tore at my heart hearing his little voice and not being able to see his face while he spoke to me. I imagined Taylor being three years old in my mind for the rest of his life, even when he was a grown man, because that was how I saw him last. He cuddled with me often and never mentioned my eyes. He just was happy that he had me captured whenever he wanted me.

I went back home the second week, feeling I was strong enough to get about in my own space. I learned a lot in that second week. I learned that people are good and want to help, that I didn't want to be a victim, that human beings adapt very quickly when the will is there, and that God could hear me.

At home in my space, I grieved. I grieved the death of my former self, a whole and healthy person. I was now handicapped and dependent. First I became depressed, and then I got angry. I became angry with God for letting another unfair thing happen to me. What had I done to deserve yet another blow when it finally seemed life was becoming a happy place for me? I had already moved forward from a heavy childhood and an uncertain youth, and I had finally built a good life. Why this now?

One particular night of sleepless darkness, I sat right up in bed and started to yell at God. I told Him how unfair this was, how sick I was of struggling and fighting, and that I refused to become a victim of tragedy. I then began to bargain with Him for a second chance. I made a deal with God, right there and then, that if He returned my sight, I would do whatever He wanted of me when I got better. I spent the rest of the night forcing my eyes to open so I could strengthen them. It was futile; the pain was too much.

During that second week, we had another snowstorm that passed like a dream for Steve and me, with us both in a semi-fog, going through the motions of living. We later discovered that various neighbors had shoveled our driveway, and others dropped off prepared meals. Flowers arrived from all over, friends came to sit with me, and I realized how meaningful the human touch can be. When you cannot see, you automatically reach out to feel with your hands so you can be connected. Every seeing person should spend a week in darkness, and then the world would learn to reach out and touch, rather than watch from a distance. I became humbled by so much support and love. I had no idea Steve and I knew so many people whose lives crossed ours.

My dear husband became a saint in my heart during those troubling days. I can only imagine the depth of his fears when he was alone. When he was around me, he was nothing but patient and giving, even when I became frustrated. I think now that he had the tougher deal, just standing by helplessly, not knowing how to make it better. But instead of tearing us down, the stress of the situation bonded us together even stronger. No matter what happened, we still wanted our life to be a good one, a united one.

Sometime in the third week, Steve and I decided to look for a second opinion. Within a few hours of discussing this idea, we called a highly respected eye surgeon who offered to see me right away. His reaction when he first looked into my eyes was "Shit." Not very promising. He told me that what I had done was the equivalent of a chemical burn – I had burned the first layer off my corneas. That, he explained, was why it was so painful when they became exposed to the air. He also told me that if I had waited one more week, I would never have opened my eyes again, as my eyeballs had started to grow onto my eyelids, thus permanently sealing them shut. I had gotten to him just in the nick of time. He put special bandage contact lens in my eyes, and he told me only time would tell. The good news was that the optic nerve had not been harmed, so the worst scenario would be a cornea transplant, which he specialized in. He also told me that the human body was an incredible piece of machinery, and it could heal itself almost miraculously. I left feeling a little more uplifted.

Within a few more weeks, the hopeless became hopeful, and as the good doctor had said, a miraculous recovery began. At first I could open my eyes in small spurts, and then for longer periods. In the beginning I could see nothing, but then I could see shadows, and I wore dark sunglasses as the light hurt my eyes. I used the telephone pad as my gauge for how I had improved. Where a week ago I had seen only foggy blobs, I could now make out the buttons if I sat right over them. Within a few more weeks, I could make out the numbers on the telephone enough to dial it myself. I went from being led around, to being driven to stores because I could see enough to shop with help.

Within one month, I could see clearly, although I looked like a vampire, as the whites of my eyes were completely bloodshot red.

Today I have perfect 20/20 vision, and I do not need glasses or lenses of any kind. I do have scar damage on parts of my cornea, but the scars do not impair my vision at all. If I get tired my eyes become very red, and I get dry eye very easily. But all in all, to look at me, no one would suspect that

I was once blind or had an eye injury. I have no scars on my face from the burns. I am a walking miracle.

My son Taylor is ten years old now, and I have another little miracle in my life – my three-year-old son Connor. His birth is another medical mystery, as I was told not to have him. But the faith I gained during my blindness taught me how strong my will is and that God does hear, so I listened to my heart and not to statistics and carried on with my pregnancy. Connor was born a healthy nine pounds, and he is perfectly normal.

Miracles are a regular occurrence in my life now. Who knew I deserved so many?

Since my bargain with God seven years ago, I have kept my end of the deal, as God did nudge me to see anew a few years after my recovery. Many aspects of my life underwent a transformation. I do less and "be" more, and I have absolute faith that I am loved and supported by whatever it is that resides in the Heavens. I don't always understand what is planned for me, but I can trust it. Challenges are not problems anymore, but opportunities for personal growth. Sounds like a giant cliché, but what doesn't kill you does make you stronger.

I live each day more aware and grateful, consciously dedicating my life and work to creating more beauty and goodness in this world. I am now a writer, artist, and many other things that I discovered and uncovered about who I am and the life I create. I see Spirit's guidance more clearly, and the divine beauty that is this experience we call life. I know nothing is an accident, there are such things as angels, and prayers are real.

~Marianne Bai-Woo

A Lion's Heart

Dreams are illustrations ... from the book
your soul is writing about you.
– Marsha Norman

A few years ago I had an extremely vivid dream. A lion trapped in a cage was in a terrible rage because of all his wasted potential. He pulled at the bars, trying to escape, managing only to bend them a little. Clearly, the lion would never be able to escape that way, yet he would die from frustration, rage, and heartbreak if he stayed in the cage.

Then with a startling clarity, I knew the lion was me. I consciously went into my dream, calmed the lion, then persuaded him to turn around and check all aspects of the cage for a way out. Moving to the other side of the cage, we discovered the door wasn't actually locked, so the lion simply pushed his claw on the latch, and he was free. Together we walked out of the prison. Surprisingly, we felt frightened to be free. We thought, "Who will look after us (for now we'd merged in the dream), and who would bring us food and provide shelter?"

To our right was a platform painted institutional green, and on it only a microphone on a stand. The lion walked up on to the platform and began telling his story. As he spoke, he could feel his heart expanding and his healing beginning. People began to gather around. They laughed and cried while he talked, and when he stopped, they came up and hugged him. The lion was happy there, but he knew it was time now to go home, reflect on this experience, and write about it. We went home to my apartment and I woke up, stunned by the implications of my dream.

There were two things that really struck me – not the fact that I was in a cage, because I had been more or less aware of that for some time – but the anger that began to wash over me as I relived the dream. I had no idea I'd been carrying such a rage. The second thing that struck me was that I was my own jailer. There was no one to blame for my imprisonment but me, and in fact, not even me, because I was simply operating under an illusion. There was absolutely no one to blame! The prison had been my choice.

At the time, I was working as a part-time ESL (English as a Second Language) teacher. I was extremely unfulfilled and frustrated, not only because of the educational system, or because I was eking out a meager living, but because I was not doing the writing that was so dear to my heart. My health was deteriorating as a result. I knew my dream had been a warning that I needed take action, but fear of 'leaving the cage' still held me back.

A few months later, another, less gentle wake-up call came during an annual check-up, when my doctor noticed I was tender in the area of my ovaries and ordered a test that revealed a benign ovarian cyst. I monitored the situation by having more ultrasounds over the next year. The year after that, I was moving to a new apartment and with all I had to do, I skipped the next appointment and the next, simply ignoring my condition for the next twelve months.

It was after moving that I became exhausted and knew that something was wrong. I went for an ultrasound, which revealed the still-benign cyst was growing, and I was told that it would need to be removed.

Darlene Montgomery

The operation was to be very simple, so I went to the hospital expecting to return home later that day.

When I woke up in the recovery room, my doctor was standing over me, a concerned expression on his face. Shock and disbelief filled me as he said, "I'm sorry. You had the early stages of ovarian cancer, and you've had a hysterectomy."

I left the hospital only to develop congestion in my lungs and other complications that required antibiotics. As I lay at home in bed, it was startlingly clear that I had a decision to make: one path would lead to my death, and one to life. From that awareness I began to take stock of my life. I'd lived five decades, and I wanted to know what I had to show for those years. When I boiled it down, there were only two items on my credit sheet that really mattered – my two sons whom I loved dearly.

When contemplating the road called inertia, the one that I knew would lead to my death, I saw clearly my two sons at my funeral, one turning to the other crying, and saying, "Mom's life was so tragic." It was that vision that spurred my decision to live. That was not the legacy I wished to leave for them. In that moment I decided that I would become an example to my children of a woman who had lived life to the fullest!

When my niece in Arizona heard about my illness, she called to give me moral support. During our telephone discussion, she said she was sending me a plane ticket to come stay with her in the warm Arizona weather where I could recuperate. While there I truly began to heal, physically and emotionally. As part of that healing, I began to write my story.

In the following summer of 1995, I went to Prince Edward Island in Canada's Maritimes, where I planned to continue my writing. I also began to fulfill the other element of my lion dream by speaking to groups of young women at universities about my story. The more I did what I loved, the more my health improved, and the more freedom I felt.

In 1996, I returned to Nova Scotia for the summer to do some more writing, but when fall came, I knew I would not be returning to Toronto. I made a quick trip back to pick up whatever I could fit into my small hatchback car, said goodbye to my two grown sons, and returned to Nova Scotia where I rented an apartment, set up my computer, and began to finish writing my story. My initial euphoria wore off quickly as I became restless and started to look around for something else to fulfill my vision.

I began writing for trade magazines such as *Hotelier* and *Canadian Grocer* to earn some income, and I found I really enjoyed getting out and meeting people. Eventually my dream began to take on a whole new life when I got involved in the field of professional speaking. I had attended three meetings of the Canadian Association of Professional Speakers back in Toronto where I connected with some interested people from Halifax, Nova Scotia, so I decided to start a branch of the association there.

I couldn't really understand what was happening to me. I'd gone to Nova Scotia to get away from it all, to follow a life-long dream and simply write, yet here I was more involved and more active than I'd ever been. And what's more, I was getting into the public speaking business and creating a newsletter for professional speakers! Initially I wondered if I was venturing off the path that I had seen in my dream, but I eventually realized this businesswoman was a very strong part of my identity, and expressing that aspect of myself was as important as writing or speaking.

After three lovely yet lonely years in Nova Scotia, I returned to Toronto, started a coaching business, opened up a speaker's bureau called Speakers Gold, and put my newsletter online. The lion in me has learned to love freedom and the gifts that it brings. Since my 'wake-up' dream,

I've written three books, published more than 200 articles, and ghostwritten another book on nutrition. I've learned that life is a gift that we are given so that we can give back, and that assisting others on their path is an integral part of my own mission. Now my life is truly exciting. I feel certain that when I have fulfilled my life sojourn, my two sons will turn to each other and say, "Wow! Our Mom was amazing!"

~ *Cathleen Fillmore*

Mastery

Maketh mine the Eye of the Eagle
Discerning, revealing,
 Encompassing all

Maketh mine the Heart of the Warrior
Unflinching, undaunted,
Courageously full

Maketh mine the Manner of the Deer
With gentleness and grace
So swift and so sure

Maketh mine the Dance of the Roses
Blooming, unfolding,
 So perfect and pure

~ *Janine Gwendoline Smith*

The Good Girl

I was six years old in October of 1956, as I stood on the balcony of our apartment building in Budapest, Hungary, watching with terror and utter confusion the rumbling approach of Russian tanks heading up the road toward the apartment where I lived with my parents and sister. That night, when I saw the expression of intense fear on the faces of my parents, I made a decision that governed my life for many years afterward. I chose to shoulder the burden of my fears rather than calling out to them. And it was then that I made a commitment to myself to be 'good' in order to be loved and accepted.

One month later, having been told only that a new doll would be awaiting me in a new country, I left behind all that I had known as home, safety, and love. My sister and I were bundled in layers of clothes, so many that we could barely move our arms, and in the early morning hours, the four of us ventured out onto a sidewalk sprinkled with a frosting of snow. I remember the depth of sorrow I felt at seeing the faces of my grandparents with tears in their eyes looking out through the window of our apartment and realizing we might never see them again. My grandmother had been the greatest source of love in my life, and it broke my heart to see her waving farewell to me.

My mother sobbed as the train moved along the tracks toward the town where we would make our escape from Hungary. Not wanting to alarm my sister and me, she claimed to have a bad cold. While we made our way through the farmer's field in the darkness of night's cover, we threw ourselves down in the mud over and over again to avoid being seen by the light of the flares the Russians shot into the sky so that they could capture or perhaps shoot those who tried to escape.

Finally we made our way to safety and to the boat that would take us to freedom and Canada, our new home. With my mask of good girl cemented well in place, I learned to survive many terrifying experiences after arriving in a strange new country where so many things were unfamiliar and where the people spoke a language I didn't understand. I recall sitting in my first kindergarten class having no way to connect with my classmates and feeling the pain of being totally alone.

My first meaningful friendship was with Wendy, with whom I experienced the elation of finally being accepted and the joy of being invited to a real Canadian home where I experienced the traditions of family living and customs. Eventually I mastered the English language and went on to high school, where I became part of the social scene. I was determined to fit in and to forget the lost, lonely little girl who'd come from Hungary. I found the confidence that moved me into circles with the 'in girls.' We sat together in the cafeteria and huddled together at school dances. With my newfound self-assurance, I even dared to ask a young man I liked to the Sadie Hawkins dance.

In 1971, I started a new chapter in my life when I married that same young man and began a teaching career at the same time. Without consideration of self, I danced through my marriage, eventually moving into the role of Super Mom to our two wonderful sons. My mask held tight as I simply ran on 'automatic' for the next 27 years without ever stopping long enough to consider how I felt or what my dreams really looked like.

Sometime around 1998, I became painfully aware that something was missing from my life. I had been feeling very lonely in my marriage, and although I couldn't put my finger on it, I knew that there was little connection left between my husband and myself. In my search for something to bring meaning into my life, I came across the ideas of Neal Donald Walsch's *Conversations with God* books, and I started attending group studies based on his writings. For the first time in thirty years, I felt passionate about something.

The more I stepped into my newfound spiritualism, the more distance I felt from my husband and my life as a whole. One day, while standing in line in a bookstore, observing a couple in front of me discussing with delight the prospect of sharing a book they were purchasing, I was struck by the emptiness of my own relationship and broke into tears. Soon after, when my youngest son moved out of our home, I decided it was time for me to leave my marriage.

Then one day in May 2000, when a friend inquired about my plans for teaching the following year, I heard myself say, "I won't be teaching next year!" I was as surprised as she was at the firm and certain tone in my response.

I was at a Shadow Processing Workshop when I was shocked into the reality that I am today. The process includes revealing those parts of our selves that we have hidden in order to prevent being abandoned, unloved, or unsafe with our primary caregivers.

I experienced myself cracking open for the first time. Slowly and meaningfully, layer by layer, I began the amazing process of removing my 'good girl' mask. I discovered that the ready smile I'd worn for years was a façade behind which I hid all my true feelings of fear, separation, loneliness, anger, and unworthiness.

In a powerful release, the floodgates opened, and I allowed a lifetime of tears and sorrow to be released. As my mask slowly came loose, I found beneath a stranger that I had never met before. With my newfound authenticity, I began to choose what good girls don't choose. And as I began to take care of myself and my own well-being, the anxiety attacks I'd been experiencing for some years began to subside.

Today I sit by my computer looking out my window-lined apartment that overlooks the ocean and the magnificence of the snow-capped mountains. I love my apartment, although it is tiny in comparison to any home I have known.

I spend time each day listening to 'What would Kati like now?' From time to time, I check in with how I feel, knowing that if it is not peaceful, I can choose again. I have completed my credentials as an *Essentials for the Best Year of Your Life* coach with the Debbie Ford Institute for Integrative Coaching so that I can best reach out to others as I guide them in creating the life of their dreams.

Being a 'good girl' has a whole new significance to me today, for now that my mask is gone, the smile I wear is truly who I am.

~ *Kati Alexandra*

On Losing a Loved One

Remembering Eric

A spiritually optimistic point of view holds that the universe
is woven out of a fabric of love. Everything that is happening is ultimately for the good if we're willing to face it
head-on and use our adversities for soul growth.
– Joan Borysenko, Ph.D.

I'll never forget the look on his face when he saw me. I'm sure
that he never expected to see me there. He froze right in his
tracks. His big, green eyes looked like they just might pop out
of his head! There he was, my 11-year-old son, Eric, standing
among the crowd of children entering the cafeteria at his
school. It was lunchtime. From a distance, I waved. I
summoned him out of the lunch line, shaking the familiar
fast food bag that I held in my hand. As he eagerly ran toward
me with a huge grin on his face, I knew that this would be a
special time for us. As it turns out, it was one of the most
rewarding experiences I remember with my son.

It was a Wednesday morning, and probably one of the
most hectic days in my office. The telephone was ringing off
the hook, there were numerous reports due at the end of the
day, and there was also an important meeting to prepare for
that afternoon. I had not yet even had my first cup of coffee.
As I reached into my pocket, searching for my favorite mint,
I found a pink paper with a list of things that I had intended
to pick up that day at the grocery store during my lunch hour.
There were several more items to add. I turned it over only to
find that it was actually a flyer from my son's school inviting

all parents to come to the school and have lunch with their child. How could something like this have slipped my mind?

I checked my electronic calendar only to find nothing scheduled for that day besides the dreaded afternoon meeting. I guess I hadn't paid too much attention to the flyer because my son had never really been fond of things like that. But for some reason that morning, I couldn't seem to get that invitation off of my mind. I began thinking. Eric was a fifth grader and would be graduating and going to middle school the next year. This was probably going to be my last opportunity to have lunch with my son.

I panicked! Certainly, a middle schooler would not want his mother to come to his school for lunch. I checked my watch. There was still time. I could still make it. Yes, that day I would have lunch with son. So, forty-five minutes before the scheduled lunch was to begin, I shut down my computer, locked the file cabinets, and dashed out to fetch Eric's favorite double cheeseburger and fries.

The look of shock on Eric's face must have mirrored my own. This was not the same child I had sent off to school that morning. The son I dropped off at school was a very studious fifth-grader in clean, starched, navy blue slacks and a spotless, button-up white cotton dress shirt. The child that stood before me was dressed as if he were going to the gym to play ball! Although still dressed in the school uniform colors of navy blue and white, his appearance in no way resembled the little boy I had envisioned having lunch with. He sported a white mesh football jersey (with no shirt underneath), navy blue fleece shorts (three sizes too big), and a very nice, and rather large, gold hoop earring. Around his neck was a fancy gold chain with the initial "A" dangling from it. (I only hoped that it was for the grades that he intended to earn.) As it turned out, the necklace belonged to a little girl named Ashanti.

As we both recovered from the shock of seeing each other, we slowly made our way to the lunch benches. Prior to

arriving, I had feared that he would be a little too embar-
rassed to sit down and have lunch with his mother. After all,
it had been only three years earlier when he had adamantly
refused to take a picture with me at school in front of his
buddies. I prepared myself. I knew that he wouldn't be rude
to me, but thought that he might eat as quickly and quietly
as possible, and then run off to play with his friends. But as
we began spreading out our food, Eric began to tell me about
what he did in class that day. He told me about a story he had
read in his social studies book and described in detail a film
he watched about Indians. Funny, he didn't tell me how or
when he had changed his clothes. I was enjoying his company
so much that I chose not to bring it up.

As he talked, he became the little, tiny boy who always
drew a picture in pre-school to show me. He was the small
child who wanted me to kneel at his bedside at night and pray
with him. He was my young son yelling in triumph while I
clapped my hands as he rode down the street for the first time
on his two-wheeler. As he spoke, ketchup ran down the side
of his mouth and proceeded to drip onto his white mesh football jersey. He seemed to neither notice or care. Young girls
passed slowly, at first trying to get his attention, and then to
whispering and giggling as they watched him talk at full
speed, his mouth chock full of a barely chewed double
cheeseburger, so unlike the cool jock they all adored.

Although I hated for the lunch to end, we began to
gather our trash in preparation to go our separate ways. He
would go back to the playground to finish recess with his
classmates. I would go back to my office, but this time in
much better spirits. I felt so good because he actually wanted
me there.

My son was really enjoying my company as much as I was
enjoying his. He began to tell me a joke, but fell out laughing
hysterically before he could finish it. His laughter was so
contagious that I too doubled over with giggles, and we
laughed so long and so hard that I thought we would both

lose our lunch. It really didn't matter whether or not he finished the joke or if it was even funny. All that mattered was that for twenty minutes, on a Wednesday afternoon, we tuned out the entire world, my son and I, and no one else existed but us. We had made magic memories that day on the elementary school lunch benches with a $2.99 burger special. It was a rare and precious day for us.

My little boy is gone now. You see, two weeks from the date of our luncheon, the child that I had prayed for, loved, treasured, and adored, died, without warning, suddenly and silently through the night, of a massive seizure. There are no more funny stories. There are no more opportunities for me to hug him tightly and kiss his forehead. There will be no new photographs. And, as I watch his friends grow up, he will always remain that 11-year-old boy. I still talk to him. I think of him always. I miss him terribly. His memory is so precious to me. We shared many things in the short time we had together. But I'll always be thankful I took the time out for a schoolyard lunch with Eric because it was one of the most rewarding experiences in my life.

~ *Tracy Clausell-Alexander*

The Visit

May it be, oh Lord, that I seek not so much to be consoled
as to console, to be understood as to understand, to be
loved as to love. Because it is in giving oneself that one
receives; it is in forgetting oneself that one is found; it is in
pardoning that one obtains pardon.
— St. Francis of Assisi

When my wonderful sister Kathy was diagnosed with breast cancer on June 6, 2001, I was there holding her hand. Seven days later, on June 13, 2001, Kathy left us to go to a better place. As she left her tired body, I told her not to be afraid, although I myself was terrified of what was to come.

Before she left, I asked her to send us an abundance of butterflies when she arrived safely on the other side. No sooner had she left her body when a nurse from the previous floor Kathy had been on came rushing into the room with a piece of paper formed into an envelope with my sister's name on it. She said breathlessly that she was told to bring it to us. Upon opening it we found a beautiful silk butterfly.

Months passed and we all had awesome butterfly stories to share with each other. On the one-year anniversary of Kathy's passing, I was sitting in the garden at my daughter Patti's house when I saw a tiny butterfly grazing on flowers around me. I decided to try something, so I said very quietly, "OK, sis, if that is you, please fly over and land on my foot." As my grandson A.J. walked out of the door, to my amazement, the butterfly landed on my foot. A.J. smiled and said, "That must be Aunt Kathy!"

With tears of happiness in my eyes, I smiled and said, "For sure."

A.J. then returned to the house and she flew away. I watched her go and said out loud, "OK, Sis, let's do this again … please land on my toe!"

She headed for my big toe, again, just as A.J. came out the door! We sat and watched as this beautiful little creature walked around my toe and shared an hour of her busy time with us. It was wonderful to see my grandson's eyes widen with awe as he watched her go slowly around my toe and my foot … then she left! It was not an easy chore for him to get me to leave that garden and get on with my day. I wanted to stay and bask in the feeling forever.

It just happened that A.J. was having a "sleepover" at my house that night, and on the way he said, "Wouldn't it be great if we had a huge butterfly on your deck in the morning, Gram?"

"We will see what Kathy has planned for us," I replied.

I went to my bed feeling peaceful that night, giving thanks too for the precious moments I shared with my sister. The next morning, when I was relaxing with my coffee, my friend Dorothy appeared at my door with a smile and a parcel! A.J. was still asleep, so I suggested we go sit on the porch, but she said, "In a minute, if you don't mind. I have something I want you to open in here. It's for your deck."

Our voices had awoken A.J., who wandered out to see what we were doing. When Dorothy unwrapped the package, we found it was a BIG brass butterfly wind chime. A.J. just pulled the covers over his head and said, "Oh my God!"

I have never been one to dread the "anniversary" of a loved one's passing. Instead, I have always done something on that day that would make them happy such as planting a rose bush, taking a walk, or, in my sister's case, going for a pedicure. Kathy always took wonderful care of herself, and a pedicure was one of those pampering moments she allowed herself.

Approaching the third year anniversary of Kathy's death, I was experiencing some sadness. After I woke up on Sunday, June 13, I decided to have a coffee on my deck. I began talking to my sister, telling her how much we all missed her. I asked her to send us the biggest butterfly she could muster up, and it had to be at my daughter Patti's place so we could all share it. In the background, I could hear my phone ringing, but I decided it was only 10 a.m., so they could call back. After all, I was busy putting in an order with my sis!

In the meantime, my brother dropped in. We chatted about the plans for the day, which included celebrating his birthday at Patti's. I shared with him my request for yet another butterfly from Kathy, and he said it would be awesome to receive another sign of her presence.

The phone rang again, so I decided I had better get on with my day. I picked up my messages to find several from my daughter telling me there was a huge butterfly on their back step! Apparently her husband Bob had noticed it an hour earlier, just at the time I had asked Kathy to send me a message! I hurried over, and there it was still on the step. Everyone, including the cat, had to walk over it to get outside, and even weirder, the screen door was dangerously brushing over it each time it opened.

After taking pictures of the butterfly, I suggested that we take it out to the picnic table with us. Even by 3 p.m. it still hadn't made any attempt to fly away. Sitting at the picnic table, I put my hand flat out and said quietly, "OK, sis, if this is you, climb up on the back of my hand." Across the picnic table she started her little stroll and climbed up on my hand. We were in awe of this outpouring of love from this creature. My grandson Michael played his new guitar, and his sister Jesse played her viola.

I said quietly, "OK, sis, let's walk up my arm and get on

my shoulder." To my delight, she slowly climbed to my shoulder!

Everyone was amazed at this incredible performance. My grandchildren continued to play the appropriate song for the day, "Song of Joy." Time seemed to stand still as my little angel remained on my shoulder. The creature seemed to be trembling, so I put my hand over her, and as I had three years before, told her not to be scared, and if she needed to go, she could. I thanked Kathy for the time she had shared with us. Through tears of happiness and gratitude, we watched as she began yet another flight on a never-ending journey.

~ *Carole Matthews*

Keep The Channel Open

There is a vitality, a life force,
an energy, a quickening
that is translated through you into action,
and because there is only one of you
in all of time
this expression is unique.

And if you block it, it will never exist
through any other medium,
and will be lost.
The world will not have it.

It is not your business to determine
how good it is, nor how valuable,
or how it compares with other expressions.

It is your business to keep it yours
clearly and directly,
to stay open and aware
to the urges that motivate you.

Keep the channel open.

~ *Martha Graham to Agnes DeMille, in*
Dance to the Piper & Promenade Home

The Littlest Angel

Love is what we are born with. Fear is what we learn. The spiritual journey is the unlearning of fear and prejudices and the acceptance of love back in our hearts. Love is the essential reality and our purpose on earth. To be consciously aware of it, to experience love in others and ourselves, is the meaning of life. Meaning does not lie in things. Meaning lies in us.
– Marianne Williamson

It was the winter that I taught in a small country school on the west coast of Vancouver Island. I had three grades of little people in my class, all beaming with the desire to learn all they could. One little boy named David from my grade one class wanted to learn more than all the others. His round puffy face would smile up at me, reminding me over and over that perhaps one day he would leave us. His frail, six-year-old body harbored a dreadful disease – leukemia. More often than not, he would be missing from our classroom because when he was subjected to another round of treatments, he would take his schooling in Vancouver.

All of us were so pleased, then, to have that happy little boy with us for Christmas. We decorated our classroom, practiced for the concert, and colored many pictures of Santa, snowmen, and angels. We read traditional Christmas stories, and some of the older children wrote very good ones of their own.

Two days before school let out for the three-week

Christmas holiday, I read a new story to the class. It was the story of "The Littlest Angel." This little angel had an awful time in heaven. He could not adjust to the routine. He was always in trouble, bumping into other angels, tripping over clouds, or dropping his halo. Nothing seemed to make his time easier until one celestial day an archangel suggested that the littlest angel return to earth to retrieve some items from his home. Just a few things to remind him of his past time on earth.

As I read the story, a heavenly silence fell over the class as each child became more involved in the plight of the angel. In hushed voices we discussed the story as the end of the school day drew to a close.

The following day during our regular show-and-tell time, David asked if he could share something with the class.

He sat in front of us on the old worn carpet holding a small wooden box.

"This is my first tooth," he explained. "This is a ribbon from my sister's hair, and this is my puppy's collar. My dad gave me this old key. My mom says this big coin is for good luck."

Even before he told us the purpose of the box, we all seemed to know. Shiny tears went dot-dot-dot down the faces of the other children – we were all thinking of the story of "The Littlest Angel."

"I have all these things so that when I go to heaven I won't be scared. Maybe you guys could make a picture for me to take so I will always remember you."

The rest of the day was spent doing just that. Each of us prepared a picture, folded it carefully, and placed it in David's wooden box.

The day ended with all of us saying goodbye to each other. Everyone gave David a special hug and received a beautiful smile in return. I went home that day with the memory of a little boy who fought his disease bravely and would one day accept his destiny.

When the holidays came to a close, we all returned to our class – all except David. He had died over Christmas in a hospital, clutching the wooden box that held his hopes and memories and ours.

I have never forgotten him. I am sure many of the students from that class, now grown with youngsters of their own, also remember "The Littlest Angel" – and the gifts of love he gave to us all.

~Brenda Mallory

The Gift of Miracles

Reach high, for stars lie hidden in your soul.
Dream deep, for every dream precedes the goal.
What e're our task, be this our creed:
We are all on this Earth to fill a need.
- Anonymous

When the phone rang, I was at my desk, preparing for the next drama class I was to teach at the Academy of Performing Arts. "It's cancer," my sister Debbie said. "The doctors told him to go home, drink his best wine, and enjoy what was left of his life. There is absolutely nothing that can be done to save Dad. He'll die within three weeks."

I was shaken to my soul with grief. Then the anger set in. How could these doctors just write off my dad like this? This was my dad, whom I adored and worshiped. My father couldn't possibly have cancer. He was a farmer, healthy and robust. He had always eaten well, including lots of fruits and vegetables we grew ourselves. His one indulgence was a glass of red wine at dinner, made from the grapes of his own vineyards. He worked the farm daily in the fresh air, getting plenty of exercise.

My mind reviewed all the special moments I had shared with my dad. I was the oldest of five children, growing up on a farm that boasted grapes, walnuts, cattle, and us kids. My parents worked from five in the morning, when the first rooster crowed, until seven at night, when the last lamb had been put in the barn. My father taught us the value of hard work and the pride it reaped.

I can still hear him in the morning, climbing the stairs to wake us, whistling happily and announcing, "Wake up, sleepy heads, it is a *beautiful* day!" He would lift us onto the caterpillar tractor to plow the fields with him. When we were older, he taught us how to drive. In the springtime, he'd find baby jackrabbits whose mothers had been killed. He would stop the tractor, put the bunnies in his coat pocket, and bring them home for us to raise until they were old enough to fend for themselves.

He was so strong that when we were young, he could lift my sisters and me from the floor with one finger. If anything broke, he could fix it. He would saddle the horses for us, tighten our wire ski bindings, and make us a special concoction of warm, sweet milk with bread when we were sick.

He'd pile all seven of us in the Willy jeep, and drive straight up our steep hill for a picnic. Being on an adventure with my dad was better than being at Disneyland. I remembered how he cried when he walked me down the aisle on my wedding day, and how, at the funeral of my sixteen-year-old brother, David, he supported my mom and the rest of us who were near collapse. He was our tower of strength, our lion in winter, our gentle, patient, loving father. He was only sixty-three years old, still madly in love with my mom after forty-two years of marriage, and grandfather to eleven grandchildren whom he treasured as he had us.

I determined right then and there that my father was not going to die. Not now! Not until we had tried everything. His doctors had said that surgery was impossible, but I had to find out all the treatment options.

I decided to take charge. These were the days before the Internet, so I had to do my research the old-fashioned way. At the library, I checked out every book on cancer. I bought books and tapes by many authors, including Bernie Siegel, Gerald Jampolsky, Shakti Gawain, and Wayne Dyer. I called everyone I thought might be able to help, asking for information. I wanted experts and answers, and we had no time to lose. Then the miracles began.

One friend told me about the 800 Cancer hotline. Another told me about cancer societies, the Physician's Data Query (PDQ), research centers, and medical schools. I studied laughter therapy and was encouraged by the work of Norman Cousins, best-selling author of the book, *Anatomy of an Illness*. Our first miracle occurred when my girlfriend Eileen was able to schedule a private appointment free of charge with the renowned laughter guru. Norman Cousins had cured himself of a life-threatening disease by laughing. I'll never forget Mr. Cousin's words upon shaking my father's hand: "I can see you are a winner. You can beat this." My dad grinned from ear to ear and responded, "Yes, I can."

We began our own therapy of positive thinking, mind over matter, and laughter. Every day I sent my dad a funny joke to give him a good belly laugh. Doom and gloom were replaced by love and laughter.

We found three experts who agreed that my father's cancer was treatable with surgery. Now the real fight began. His national HMO insurance carrier refused to pay for any tests or surgery, saying that any treatment for his rare condition was "experimental." We gained seven "second" opinions, all stating that surgery could save my dad's life and that it was a standard procedure.

After several conversations with various insurance officers, I asked the CEO of the company why coverage was refused. He said the insurance carrier's felt it was too expensive to try to save a dying man. I was astounded! I called the CEO back and read him the press release I had written with a list of the television stations, radio stations, and major newspapers around the country that would receive this announcement that day. The press release simply stated that this HMO had decided to play God and take the life of a "simple farmer" because it would save the insurance company money. It was a portrayal of David versus Goliath, and the CEO knew his company didn't stand a chance of winning any sympathy by battling us in the press. Approval for the procedure was granted. Knowing the power of these huge conglomerations, I reckoned this was another miracle.

The night before surgery, we met with the medical team. They agreed to allow a tape recorder in the operating and recovery rooms that would play words of encouragement. My family members and I had made these special tapes. We had sung funny Italian songs and told him how much we loved him and needed him in our lives. However, we got some bad news when we arrived at the hospital. Dad had already been taken into surgery before we could say good-bye or bring him the tapes. We were confident of the surgeons' abilities and my dad's great attitude. Nevertheless, my mother feared that if Dad didn't hear the tapes, he might die.

The nurses didn't know how to get the tape recorder into the operating room, so I did something I had seen in the movies. Wearing my green sweat clothes, I placed my pager on the outside of my pants, grabbed a mask and rubber gloves from a utility closet, and marched into the surgical center as if I belonged. With an air of authority, I calmly handed the nurse my boom box with five cassettes. She set it up, and my dad had another miracle.

He was released from the hospital a week ahead of schedule, and he lived happily and healthily with my mom on the farm for three more years. He went to work and was as busy as ever, plowing fields, mending fences, whistling in the morning, and saving bunnies. He still had his glass of home-made red wine every day, and I still sent him a daily joke.

The fact that my dad lived three more grateful years instead of three weeks was a miracle – a miracle that he created because he fought for his life. Then one early November day, the cancer reappeared with a vengeance.

It was time to renew our grape contracts with the winery so Mom would be secure for the following harvest. But the wineries weren't keen on signing. For seven years, California had had little rain. The drought had nearly destroyed the grape industry. The winery representative told Dad they wanted to be fair, but "in reality, the vineyards may all be dead by next year if this drought continues." Dad responded confidently, "Don't worry. When I get to heaven, I'm going to open the flood gates, and you'll get so much rain, you won't know what to do with it."

"Al," my mom said without realizing the imminence of my dad's death, "There'll be hundreds of people at your funeral. I don't want a rainy day."

"Honey," he replied, "it's going to rain right up until my funeral, but then you watch. I'll make the sun come out, and you'll have your beautiful sunny day." The vintner signed an equitable contract, and my mom felt some relief.

I knew we were facing Dad's final days on this earth, but I didn't give up hope for one final miracle. When I asked my dad what more I could do for him in this life, he held my hands and said, "I am dying a peaceful and happy man. I married the woman I loved, and we were married for forty-five years. We had five wonderful children and eleven grandchildren, and I was lucky enough to do work that I was passionate about. I have lived my dreams."

But, he added, he had never had a chance to speak with a man he admired, Dr. Bernie Siegel, whose book *Love, Medicine & Miracles* had given him so much help. Without thinking, I retorted, "Dad, you'll get to speak to Dr. Siegel. I'll make sure of it." I left the house kicking myself, wondering how in the world I was going to make Dad's last request come true. I didn't know Dr. Siegel. I didn't know anybody who knew him. Even worse, I had no address or contact number. The only way I might possibly reach him was through his publisher. That night I wrote an impassioned plea to the name and address that I found inside the jacket cover of Bernie's book and overnight-mailed the letter to New York.

With hope in my heart and a prayer on my tongue, I turned my efforts to helping the family cope.

Dad died as he had lived, in harmony and with dignity. He died in my arms, on his farm, in his room overlooking the vineyards he had tended with love for almost fifty years. And his last wish was granted. Dr. Bernie Siegel telephoned my dad on his last day on earth. Dad had been in and out of a coma all day. I whispered in Dad's ear that Dr. Siegel was on the phone. Dad awoke, took the phone, and listened with that smile we loved so much while Dr. Siegel led him in a beautiful visualization and prayer. Dad thanked Bernie as tears streamed from everyone's eyes. Another miracle had occurred.

Small miracles? We believe so. And, yes, as Dad had predicted, it began raining less than an hour after he died. It did not stop until the day of his funeral. Then the sun shone brightly on the many hundreds of people who had gathered to celebrate the life of one farmer. The love my dad had planted and nurtured during his lifetime was reaped and harvested at his death.

Miracles do happen to those who believe in them.

~ *Cynthia Brian*

One Small Miracle

As we lived within an hour's drive of the seminar site, we hadn't thought it necessary to book a room in the hotel. I came to regret that decision when my husband Jerry began to feel ill on Saturday afternoon.

Fortunately, life smiled upon us in the form of my younger brother. We encountered him quite by chance in a crowd of 4,000 people. He promptly gave us the key to his hotel room and urged Jerry to go there and lie down.

The seminar sessions were in full swing. With the hallways and elevators nearly deserted, we were able to quickly make our way up to my brother's room. I slid the key card into the door lock without the anticipated result – no little green light, no clicking sound. I checked the room number and tried again. Still nothing. After several more frustrating tries, I concluded that the door was not going to open. Jerry was leaning against the wall, not feeling well enough to offer his usual advice or assistance. One door down, as if on cue, an older woman dressed in a soft blue pantsuit exited from her room.

She bent down to pick up a dropped book. When she stood again, I immediately recognized Carolyn, a dear friend I hadn't seen in years. Learning of our plight, and very true to form, she re-opened her door and ushered us into her room. I noted the faint smell of her trademark perfume lingering in the air as we entered.

Without bothering with any formal introductions, Jerry stretched out on the bed and was asleep within minutes. Carolyn motioned me toward the room's only comfortable chair. I noted how its swirls of soft coral fabric matched the room's window curtains. She pulled a straight back chair out from behind the desk for herself. In deference to the twenty or so years she had on me, I suggested that we trade chairs. She wouldn't hear of it.

At first, we were not unlike young girls at a slumber party, a bit giggly and full of secrets to share. Our conversation deepened before long, focused on spiritual matters. Our ever-increasing love for God had always been our bond. We were two old souls who had traveled down many roads together, in this and other lifetimes.

We talked for several hours, stopping only occasionally to munch on the goodies she had fortuitously stashed in her room. Finally, sated in both stomach and soul, we fell silent. In that moment, Jerry awoke and announced that he was once again feeling fine.

When I looked at Carolyn one last time before a parting hug, I noted her skin. It was clear and radiant in spite of her seventy years, almost translucent in quality. I've seen that look before, and I should have known what was to come.

I learned of Carolyn's death some time in the months that followed the seminar. I'd been told that she'd been sitting in a chair in her formal living room and had left gently, a final journey to the Far Country. I might have been heart-broken if it hadn't been for those special hours we'd shared at the seminar. Spirit, in one of Its mysterious ways, had given me time with her. It was a precious gift for which I remain most grateful.

Shortly after we had left Carolyn's room that afternoon at the seminar, we found my brother and returned his room key. We explained that it no longer worked and suggested that he go to the front desk for a new one. The next day, we learned that he had forgotten our cautionary words, went to his room with the original key card, and had no trouble opening the door on the first try.

Some would call it coincidence, and some would plead a

case of synchronicity. Me? I put this down as one of life's small miracles "bringing together of two friends for a final goodbye."

Small miracles have a way of letting us know that each one of us matters, that we are not alone or overlooked. We *are* cared for – absolutely.

~ *Jo Leonard*

A Garden in Brooklyn
for Marie

Her father grew massive gardens in Connecticut,
a half acre with rows of sweet corn, string beans,
    cherry tomatoes,
and sunflowers lifting their heavy heads toward
    the light,
framed in a profusion of zinnias and mums.

After he was gone, her brother kept a part of it growing,
but each year there was less time,
and the soil finally went fallow.

When she comes home on the train from Brooklyn,
she borrows her mother's car
and goes to the garden store to buy a tiny wishing well,
just twenty bucks, which no one is likely to steal.

It's for the little patch of earth
in front of the brownstone where she lives,
up three flights of creaky stairs.
She brings back bags of rich lakeside soil
to nourish the petunias trying to live
between the brick and the concrete.
They need all the help they can get, she says,
to survive when the kids playing in the street
knock the ball into the flowers,
and they have to dig it out.

What is left blooms on,
a small spot of color
on a gray street in Brooklyn.

~ *Laura Reave*

On Mothers and Daughters

The Hug

We need 4 hugs a day for survival.
We need 8 hugs a day for maintenance.
We need 12 hugs a day for growth.
– Virginia Satir

I always knew that I was different. First of all, it was the hair. My hair was very blond, almost white. My parents both had very dark hair. And then there was the face. I didn't look like either one of them. Then there was the fact that I was alone. As I looked around at other families, there were always several children with their parents. So right from an early age, I knew that I must be from some strange place like Venus, and just here for a short sojourn. But the real concern about who I was began when I started school at five years old.

For four years, I had been at home with my mother. I had no siblings, so we were alone together during the day. Then that fateful first day of school arrived when I discovered that I had to share and interact in a pleasing manner with others. I spent a lot of time in the "corner" where the teacher sent those pupils who were "bad." So not only did I not seem to belong at home, but I didn't seem to belong in the school environment either. Back at home, my parents could not understand why I couldn't fit in. Wasn't it obvious to them? My hair was different, my face was different, and I was all alone. I became quiet and retreated into an inner world where I had my inner world friends who loved me and talked to me, and I was normal there.

The first year of school finally passed, and it was now summer. It was a hot, sultry summer day when my father came to me and said that my mother could no longer look after me. He had to go to work every day, so we would have to go to live with my grandmother. What had happened? Why couldn't she look after me? Why did we have to go to a strange place? This news confirmed my worst fears. My mother didn't love me. And if she couldn't care for me and didn't love me, it was probably because I was so different and didn't really belong to them. Life as I knew it was over. I was five and I was very depressed. Where would I find love?

I withdrew from happiness. There was nothing that could be done. My mother had been diagnosed with aggressive multiple sclerosis, and her life, as she had known it, ended. Confined to a wheelchair, and with deteriorating physical and mental capacity, she needed ongoing support and care. Her support team was me and my father. It was a daunting daily task to keep the home going and make sure that Mother could manage. Tasks done with love are a pleasure, but of course I knew that she didn't love me, so each day was heavy with a sense of duty and obligation, rather than love.

The months stretched into years, and Mother's health became increasingly worse, with many months spent in hospital. Our home became a dismal place, where a crisis requiring a call to 911 always lurked around the corner. The years dragged on, and I began to search for love. There certainly appeared to be no love at home.

And then suddenly on Christmas Day, after a long spell in the hospital, my mother died. It was over, and now there was certainly no hope of ever finding love at home.

I think it was the ever-present loneliness that pushed me to seek one relationship after another. When I was thirteen, a boy named Charles carried my books home from school. That was the beginning of my long, and not so illustrious, search for love. I always looked outward to see who might want to be my friend and who could give me the loving attention I so craved. I wasn't fussy, and that proved to be a serious problem as the years went on.

But finally I met a very nice man, and we spent a lot of time together. Our relationship was fulfilling and happy, and we were married. His career in motor racing took us all over North America. It was an exciting time in my life, full of meeting new people and traveling extensively.

However, after five years of marriage, I began to feel a gnawing emptiness growing within me. I recognized this feeling. It said to me that the love in my life couldn't be real. It was an inner voice that invalidated my worthiness to receive love, and that voice drove me to search again for 'true love.' Then something happened that changed everything.

One afternoon I lay down for a little nap after work. During the nap a rather loud, but kind voice, said to me, "Barb, God is love." When I awoke, I knew that my life would never be the same again. If love is God and God is love, then my search for human love all this time had really been a search for God in my life. I asked inwardly for a spiritual guide, someone who knew how to find God. A short time after this dream I came across a teacher called the MAHANTA,* who taught me about love and our true nature as Soul. This gave life a whole new meaning; my focus was now to find the spiritual purpose of my life.

One of the ways I was helped was through understanding the meaning of events in my life. For so many years I'd held a belief that my mother hadn't loved me. It had caused me to hold a part of my heart away from life and to feel somehow separate.

I'd gone through many changes, including the separation of my partner of many years. A deep and painful healing was now taking place. Then one night in a dream, I met my mother in the inner worlds. We greeted each other and were immediately drawn together in a warm and loving hug. As we embraced, I felt her warmth, and waves of love poured through me. The waves undulated between us and in that moment, years of isolation dropped away as a tremendous realization surged up from deep within my heart. She had always loved me! It was I who had pulled away from love and isolated myself from her. My mother's love had always been there, but I hadn't been able to accept it.

This realization brought a spiritual healing, a true healing of the soul. In accepting my mother's love in this experience, I opened my heart to receive more love from others and to be able to give love more freely to those in my life. This is my spiritual purpose. I am no longer from another planet. I am here and ready to love and serve life, to feel the presence of God in every breath. Thanks, Mom!

~ *Barbara Allport*

*MAHANTA is the name for the spiritual guide of those on the path of ECKANKAR.

A Pact Made in Heaven

We never know how high we are
Till we are called to rise;
And then, if we are true to plan,
Our statures touch the skies.
– Emily Dickinson

I was in shock and disbelief as I looked at the picture I'd found in an envelope from my mother's personal effects. She and I had been very close. We shared just about everything, so discovering something that she'd kept secret from me was hard to understand. Inside the envelope were documents that revealed that my mother had given up a baby girl for adoption. I was shaken as I looked over pictures of my much younger mother holding a tiny baby. How could this be? How could my mother, my best friend, keep this secret all these years?

When I called my father for answers, he revealed that my sister was several years older than me and that she was my "full" sister. When the baby arrived, my parents were simply too young to care for an infant. My mother named her baby Sandra Lee. I realized how devastating it must have been for my mother to give up her precious infant, because when I was born eight years later, she named me Sandra Leigh as well.

I was convinced that my mother left this information for me to find. What was too painful in life would be shared in death. My father told me he hadn't known the letter or the pictures existed. I decided right then and there that I was going to find my sister if it was the last thing I ever did. Over the next few weeks, I set about gathering the necessary paperwork to begin my search.

After waiting on pins and needles for three months, I finally received the exciting call telling me that the agency had located my sister. I was elated with the news! And best of all, she was only a few hours away and willing to have some contact with me. I immediately wrote a letter to my sister explaining who I was and filling her in on other details about our family.

Two weeks later, I was in my car when my cell phone rang. I nearly drove off the road when the voice on the other end said, "Hi, Sandra. It's your sister calling." The tears streamed down my face as we spoke for about twenty minutes, trying to fill in the empty spaces and the question marks. From that day forward we began to form our friendship, and three months later we decided to meet face to face. I can't recall ever being as emotional.

As I approached the little town of Dashwood and pulled into the driveway of my sister's home, I realized that our meeting would change the rest of my life.

I walked in the house and before I got to where she was standing, I was crying uncontrollably. Here was the spitting image of my mother standing in front of me! We spent the next twelve hours talking, eating, laughing and sharing. It was the most amazing day of my life.

During that afternoon we discovered that our mothers shared some amazing similarities. Both had a joy for life, an infectious laugh, and a twinkle in their eye. So many positive similarities and yet there were the negative ones too. My mother died from cancer, and her mother was dying of cancer as we spoke. Here were two women who put the world on their shoulders and were selfless beyond belief. They would always lend an ear to someone else, but never, ever shared their own grief, their pain, their secrets, or their dreams, all of which took a toll, I am sure. The summer came and went, and my sister and I were getting closer and closer.

As each month went by, I wished I could meet her mother. I wanted to know this wonderful person who'd adopted my sister. On Labor Day weekend my whole family came to Dashwood to meet my sister. To my delight, who should I see walking up the driveway, but my sister's mother! What a brave soul she was to show up unannounced to meet her daughter's newfound family. It was a wonderful day. We talked and we laughed, and when she was too tired, she laid down for a nap. She decided to return home after dinner, and we had a tearful goodbye. How was I to know that would be the first and last time I would ever see her?

Two weeks later I received a phone call from my sister that her mother had been admitted to hospital and was failing fast. I gave her all the support I could, having just gone through this almost a year earlier. A few days later she succumbed to her illness, the same illness that stole my mother from me.

How could this happen? Was the world this cruel? Or was it the perfect timing of fate? I had lost my mother, but gained the sister I had wished for my whole life. She had lost her mother, but gained a family she had been secretly yearning for her entire life. Sometimes I think this reunion was planned long before we ever came to this lifetime. A plan was devised from somewhere very far away.

Is it possible that two souls made a pact to come into this lifetime and share the upbringing of two little girls, and when these girls needed each other the most, the opportunity would arise for them to meet? It may seem a little far-fetched, but somehow it's the only way for me to accept the loss of my mother. It's the only way to explain how two such amazing women were taken from their families long before it was time for them to go.

Sometimes I have a dream at night, and in it I see two women standing side by side and holding hands, looking down on two women standing side by side and saying to each other, "We did a good job, didn't we!"

~ *Sandra Irvine*

Coming Home to Oz

One night many years ago, when I was expecting my second child, I had a dream, which, in retrospect, can only be called prophetic. I opened my eyes to see an old man sitting at the end of my bed. He had an air of wisdom about him, and he wanted to talk about the child to whom I would soon give birth. He asked whether I wanted a boy or a girl, but when I said that I already had a daughter and would therefore like a boy, he replied, "Well, I am sending you a girl, a very troubled girl who needs a strong family. She will need your guidance." He went on to explain that my child was an old soul who had been very badly abused in a past life and that she was coming to me to learn to trust herself and other people. Our conversation continued for some time, and when I awoke in the morning I remarked to myself on what a strange dream it had been. It had seemed so real.

My second daughter, Eve, was born on a lovely summer's day, on July 8, 1984. In spite of the dream, she was extremely easy baby. She slept through the night by six weeks of age and hardly ever cried. Born at 8 pounds, 10 ounces, she continued to grow into a pleasant, cherubic baby, with the appetite of a horse. Our friends found it amusing to see how much our little baby could consume. I didn't know then how ironic that detail would turn out to be.

As Eve grew older, there was a beautiful ethereal quality about her, as though she was in this world and yet not fully of it. She developed into a gifted artist who was also very intelligent and who excelled in mathematics, eventually placing third in a provincial mathematics competition. Amidst all of these blessings, the warning of my dream was forgotten until Eve's fourteenth year.

That year was an incredibly difficult one for our family. My husband suffered a very serious break to his leg and was unable to work for seven months. Because we had depended solely on his income, I found myself suddenly scrambling to get work in order to sustain our family of five.

That same year, both of my parents were admitted to separate hospitals, my father for heart problems and my mother for a hip replacement that developed complications. My energy was so consumed with running from one hospital to the other, dealing with the financial strain and daily stress at home, that at first I did not notice the changes in Eve, who had slowly and subtly gone from her happy, chatty self, to a withdrawn and silent child. But when she developed strange eating habits, became obsessive about fat content, and began exercising constantly, I started to be concerned. I took her to our family doctor, but he dismissed my worries and told me I was just being silly. 'Maybe he's right,' I thought. 'Perhaps I'm just overreacting.' But in my heart I knew that something was wrong.

Eve continued to lose weight over the following months. Even my friends were beginning to notice, and I would sometimes find her exercising in her bedroom in the middle of the night. But again, when I took her to a specialist on eating disorders, I was told that Eve was a lovely, slim girl and that I had no need to worry. Reassured, I again turned my attention back to my parents, whose health went into further decline. I was virtually living at two hospitals, with little time to pay attention to the situation at home. It was winter then, and it seemed that Eve was at home as rarely as I was.

When warmer weather finally arrived, our family decided to spend the first holiday weekend at our cottage, a three-hour drive from the city. It had been a long, hard winter, and we were looking forward to this time away. The weather was fabulous, and it felt great to be free of winter's bundled layers.

I was outside enjoying the sun when Eve appeared on the dock in her bathing suit. As I glanced up and saw her, my heart constricted. 'Oh my God!' I thought, 'How could I have been so blind?' She looked like a skeleton, her bones protruding through her skin, her feet noticeably purple from lack of circulation. I discovered later that Eve, who was 5' 4 inches tall, weighed only 82 pounds!

Shocked and alarmed, my husband and I packed the children right back into the car and headed straight for Toronto's Sick Kids Hospital, the only hospital in our area known to have a program for eating disorders. As Eve was admitted to the Eating Disorder Ward, a mixture of relief, fear, guilt, and anger swept through me, followed by a horrible sadness. How could I have been such a bad parent? I berated myself. I was extremely grateful to think that Eve was now getting the help she needed, but how had I failed to notice that my daughter was starving herself to death? After she was admitted, I sat in my car in the hospital parking lot and sobbed for hours. This event was to mark the beginning of an intensely dark time in my life.

The next day my family was interviewed by a team of psychiatrists, three of them behind one-way mirrors. They watched to see how we interacted and what our family dynamics were. I was willing to do anything to help my child get well, but having to submit to this type of scrutiny, on top of everything we were already going through, was unbearable to me, not to mention how difficult it was for my other two children. Finally, we were informed that Eve would not be released until her weight had reached one hundred pounds. I felt like I was falling apart.

Slowly, over time, Eve's weight started to climb, but I began to realize that she was still not getting well, mentally or emotionally. The hospital ward was an unhealthy place, more like a jail where the inmates were force-fed, and the kids taught each other brilliant tricks to avoid eating. However, during her stay, I did learn a lot about Eve's disease. Most importantly, I learned that anorexia isn't really about food, but about control and self-worth.

I waited for Eve to reach her target weight so that I could regain control over my child's healing. Finally, after eight weeks, Eve's weight hit one hundred pounds, and she was released from the hospital. This was a monumental achievement; however, other parents at the hospital warned me that the real roller coaster ride was now about to begin.

The hospital therapist had told me that Eve was depressed and recommended that she go on anti-depressants, but I resisted this, feeling that it would only mask the real problem. After she was released, I found an excellent therapist for her and was confident that we would finally get to the bottom of the problem. Eve's weight did eventually become acceptable, yet she remained incredibly distant. Sometimes I would find her in tears, still so sad. I loved her so much, but I was at a loss as to how I could help this precious soul to gain the trust and self-worth she would need to get fully well.

During this entire ordeal, I prayed daily for guidance and strength. More than anything, I wanted my child to be well. I wanted her to know her own worth and to experience joy in her life once again. At one point during this period, my youngest daughter, Emma, drew me a picture of a heart filled with four circles: one labeled "Hope," another "Courage," the other, "Pride," and the last, "Strength." This act of love from my ten-year-old lifted my spirits immensely and gave me the courage to continue battling the demon that had been ripping our lives apart. I still have the picture hanging framed in my room.

That summer Eve was booked as crew on a ship for two weeks. I felt hopeful that this could be a turning point for her, but then the day before she was to leave, I found marks on her arms showing that she'd been cutting herself. I became hysterical and refused to let her go on the trip because I was terrified she would throw herself overboard in the dark of night. She pleaded with me to let her go and, after speaking to her therapist, who felt that the sun and exercise would be good for Eve, I hesitantly agreed.

When Eve returned from her holiday, I knew we had to try something different. It was time to admit that she needed antidepressants. We found a new doctor who could prescribe the medication Eve needed, and once she began taking the antidepressants, she did start to improve a bit, attending school more regularly and getting more involved with life – but she still wasn't happy. At this point I had tried everything I could, but she remained distant, hardly talking, and coming and going like a shadow. I knew that I was still treating her like a sick child and that I needed to learn to trust her again if I was ever to help her trust herself, but I didn't know how to do it.

Meanwhile, life went on for the rest of us. My youngest daughter, Emma, had been taking riding lessons, and I regularly drove her to the riding stables. I began to spend a lot of time around the barns, and it was there that I remembered my long-forgotten love for horses, which had begun over thirty years before, when my father owned a farm. It was while I was hanging around the barn, waiting for Emma, that I heard about a horseback riding program for beginners. Suddenly, I got the idea to sign Eve and myself up for lessons. I would share my own love of horses with her!

The first few times Eve and I drove to the stable, the air between us was very strained. I tried desperately to have a conversation with my daughter, but I received only single word responses, so I eventually resorted to the radio. Soon, however, we were riding regularly, and I began to notice a change in Eve. For the first time in many years, she was excited about something. And then, after a few sessions, a funny thing started to happen. Eve fell in love with riding, becoming as passionate about it as her sister Emma and I were. Our car rides were now spent chatting excitedly about horses and riding. What's more, Eve started to laugh again! It's amazing what a miracle a smile can be. For us, it was tangible proof that the deeper healing process was finally underway.

Eventually, we made the decision to buy our own horse. I figured that the cost was about the same as the therapy, and we got far more back in return. This horse, which we named the Wizard of Oz, is one of the most magical things to have happened in Eve's life. Riding Oz has given her a great sense of empowerment and love in her life, which has led to an incredible transformation. Oz is a source of love for her, and just as importantly, he provides an opportunity for her to give unconditional love to another being. On the days that she rides him, she gets to the barn extra early and spends over an hour brushing his coat. When they are finished riding, she always takes him to the best patches of grass to graze. It doesn't matter if it is pouring rain; she makes sure that he gets this special time.

Eve has been riding for two years now, and she is a changed person. Through her time with Oz, she has learned not only to control her own emotional responses in order to be a better rider, but to trust and give the reins over to her horse when necessary, just as we must surrender to life once we have done all that we must do. In finding her rhythm with Oz, she has regained the rhyme and rhythm of her own life. She has graduated from college, and she is living on her own, a young woman full of joy, passion, and purpose. It was a long, difficult journey, but the real inner healing began with love – Eve's love of riding and her love for a horse – which helped show her the way home to herself.

~ *Christine Switzer*

Lord Make Me An Instrument

Lord, make me an instrument of Thy peace.
Where there is hatred, let me sow love;
Where there is injury, pardon;
Where there is doubt, faith;
Where there is despair, hope;
Where there is darkness, light;
Where there is sadness, joy.
O Divine Master, grant that I may not so much seek
To be consoled as to console,
To be understood as to understand,
To be loved as to love.
For it is in giving that we receive;
It is in pardoning that we are pardoned;
It is in dying to self that we are born to eternal life.

~ *Saint Francis of Assisi*

Creating Our Reality

The longer I live, the more I realize the impact of attitude on life. Attitude to me is more important than facts. It is more important than the past, than education, than money, than circumstances, than failures, than success, than what other people think, say, or do. It is more important than appearance, gift, or skill. It will make or break a company … a church … a home.

The remarkable thing is we have a choice every day regarding the attitude we will embrace for that day. We cannot change our past … The only thing we can do is play on the string we have, and that is our attitude. I am convinced that life is 10% what happens to me and 90% how I react to it. And so it is with you … We are in charge of our attitudes.

– Charles Swindoll

If You Were Really Important

Spiritual progress is like detoxification.
Things have to come up in order to be released.
Once we have asked to be healed, then our unhealed
places are forced to the surface.
— Marianne Williamson

It was a simple assignment ... just off the top of my head. I didn't realize how powerful it was.

In one of my workshops, I instructed all my students to "expand the bottom line" by participating full out in their jobs for one entire week. Novel idea! They were to "act-as-if" their actions really made a difference to everyone around them. The key question they were to constantly ask themselves throughout each day was "If I were really important here, what would I be doing?" And then they were to set about "doing it."

Peggy, sitting in the third row, resisted the assignment. She lamented that she hated her job and was just biding her time until she found a new one. Each day was pure drudgery as she watched the clock slowly move through the eight painful hours. With great skepticism, she finally agreed to try it for just one week – to expand her bottom line by committing 100 percent to her job, knowing that she really counted.

The following week, as I watched Peggy walk into the room, I couldn't believe the difference in her energy level. When I asked her what was going on, she excitedly reported the events of her week:

"My first step was to brighten up the dismal office with some plants and posters. I then started to really pay attention to the people I work with. If someone seemed unhappy, I asked if there was anything wrong and if I could help. If I went out for coffee, I always asked if there was anything I could bring back for the others. I complimented people. I invited two people for lunch. I told the boss something wonderful about one of my co-workers. (Usually I'm selling myself!)

"Then I asked myself how I could improve things for the company itself. First I stopped complaining about the job – I realized I was such a nag! I became a self-starter and came up with a few very good ideas which I began implementing. Every day I made a list of things I wanted to accomplish, and I set about accomplishing them. I was really surprised by how much I could do in a day when I focused on what I was doing! I also noticed how fast the day went by when I was involved.

"I put a sign on my desk that said, 'If I were really important here, what would I be doing?'

"And every time I started to fall back into my old patterns of boredom and complaining, the sign reminded me of what I was supposed to be doing. That really helped.

"It is amazing to me that by just asking myself this question, I was able to create such a great work experience for myself ... and for everybody else!"

What a difference a simple expansion of the bottom line made in just one short week! It made Peggy feel connected to everyone and everything around her – including the organization itself. And it allowed her to enjoy her job for the first time since she had been hired.

While she knew it would soon be time to move on to another job, she realized that while she was still there it was in everyone's best interest, particularly her own, to create an environment of commitment and caring. After all, who wants to spend their days in an energy filled with alienation, boredom and negativity? (I would find it strange if anyone answered YES to that question!) It is also worth noting that with such positive energy, the likelihood of Peggy getting a great recommendation and finding a new, more challenging job would be greatly increased.

I hope Peggy's story has convinced each and every one of you to "act-as-if you were really important" in all aspects of your own lives. Trust me when I tell you that there will come a day when you discover you don't have to "act-as-if" any more. Why? Because you finally realize YOU TRULY ARE IMPORTANT! No acting required!

~ *Susan Jeffers, Ph.D.*

Glenna's Goal Book

In 1971 I was a single mother with three young daughters, a house payment, a car payment, and a need to rekindle some dreams.

One evening I attended a seminar and heard a man speak on the l x V = R Principle (Imagination mixed with Vividness becomes Reality). The speaker pointed out that the mind thinks in pictures, not in words, and as we vividly picture in our mind what we desire, it will become a reality.

This concept struck a chord of creativity in my heart. I knew the biblical truth that the Lord gives us "the desires of our heart" (Psalms 37:4) and that "as a man thinketh in his heart, so is he" (Proverbs 23:7). I was determined to take my written prayer list and turn it into pictures. I began cutting up old magazines and gathering pictures that depicted the "desires of my heart." I arranged them in an expensive photo album and waited expectantly.

I was very specific with my pictures. They included:
- A good-looking man
- A woman in a wedding gown and a man in a tuxedo
- Bouquets of flowers (I'm a romantic.)
- Beautiful diamond jewelry (I rationalized that God loved David and Solomon, and they were two of the richest men that ever lived.)
- An island in the sparkling blue Caribbean
- A lovely home
- New furniture
- A woman who recently became president of a large corporation (I was working for a company that had no

female officers. I wanted to be the first woman to be president of the company.)

About eight weeks later, I was driving down a California freeway, minding my own business at 10:30 in the morning. Suddenly a gorgeous red-and-white Cadillac passed me. I looked at the car because it was a beautiful car. And the driver looked at me and smiled. I smiled back because I always smile. Now I was in deep trouble. Have you ever done that? I tried to pretend that I hadn't looked. "Who me? I didn't look at you?" He followed me for the next fifteen miles. Scared me to death! I drove a few miles, he drove a few miles. I parked, he parked … . And eventually I married him!

On the first day after our first date, Jim sent me a dozen roses. Then I found out that he had a hobby. His hobby was collecting diamonds. Big ones! And he was looking for somebody to decorate. I volunteered! We dated for about two years, and every Monday morning I received a long-stemmed red rose and a love note from him.

About three months before we were to be married, Jim said to me, "I have found the perfect place to go on our honeymoon. We will go to St. John's Island down in the Caribbean." I laughingly said, "I never would have thought of that!"

I did not confess the truth about my picture book until Jim and I had been married for almost a year. It was then that we were moving into our gorgeous new home and furnishing it with the elegant furniture that I had pictured. (Jim turned out to be the West Coast wholesale distributor of one of the finest eastern furniture manufacturers.)

By the way, the wedding was in Laguna Beach, California, and included the gown and tuxedo as realities. Eight months after I created my dream book, I became the vice president of the human resources company where I worked.

Decide what it is that you want in every area of your life. Imagine it vividly. Then act on your desires by actually constructing your personal goal book. Convert your ideas into concrete realities through this simple exercise. There are no impossible dreams. And remember, God has promised to give his children the desires of their heart.

~ *Glenna Salsbury*
From *Chicken Soup for the Soul Book 1*

Shield of Protection

Five years ago, I was driving along a road when suddenly my car hit something, then sprang into the air, heading straight towards the glass wall of a building. To my horror, my car crashed through the wall and I died! Just then I woke up and realized I had been dreaming.

Five years later, I had another similar dream. Again, I was driving my car when I crashed into and through a wall. As the car came to a stop, I realized to my relief and delight that I was still alive.

As I looked around to survey the scene, I saw pieces of glass falling around me, but not on me. Glancing upward, to my amazement I saw a silver metal shield suspended in the air above my head, protecting me from the falling glass. While still in the dream, I recalled the dream of five years before and realized that because I had already died once before, I was protected, and I didn't need to experience dying again.

In my spiritual search, I had come upon ECKANKAR, a path of direct experience with Spirit. In ECKANKAR, dreams are used to assist seekers on their spiritual journey, and they serve as a way to work out unnecessary karma. Dreams play an integral role in my life, giving me guidance and protection.

I felt that I had received a gift of working out karma in the dream five years ago, and therefore was protected in this accident. I then awoke and recorded my dream in my journal.

Two weeks later, my girlfriend and I were on our way to

my mum's home. We were driving southbound on a sixty-kilometer-an-hour road when up ahead I saw two cars approaching, one behind the other. I could hear the revving sound of their engines as they sped to pass one another while heading towards us at an incredible speed. When one car pulled into the center lane to pass the other, a disquieting feeling told me we could be in danger. My inner voice said to hold on, be cautious, be alert, and be prepared to pull into the ditch if I needed to.

I held my breath as the cars raced closer towards us, then sped past us. My eyes immediately went to my rear-view mirror, and what I saw is etched forever in my memory. The passing car crashed head on into an SUV driving directly behind me, then spun out of control, while pieces of debris flew through the air.

I quickly stopped my car, then called 911 on my cell phone as we ran towards the accident. Drawing closer, I saw the driver of the car, slumped on the front seat, bleeding and completely still. A crowd of people started gathering around the accident scene. Someone yelled out, "He's breathing!" Another reported that the family in the SUV was okay.

Finally the police arrived, directing the small crowd to move back and to stay to be questioned. As the officer opened the door to the back seat, I was shocked to see there was another passenger in the car whose body was covered by a sheet, a sign that the person hadn't made it out alive. By then an air ambulance had arrived to transport the injured driver to the hospital, but it was too late. He had also died.

By now I was shaking inside, all too aware that it could have been our car that had been demolished. There had been a mere two-second difference from our car to the SUV. As I gave the details to the police officer, he said emphatically, over and over, "You are very lucky! You are *very* lucky!" Because of the size of their vehicle, the family in the SUV had not been hurt, he told me.

Darlene Montgomery

Then eyeing my small, low-to-the-ground car, he said, "Your car would have been crushed, and you would be *dead*!" His words silenced my thoughts.

My friend and I proceeded to my mum's, where we tried to calm ourselves before heading home. On the way back, I drove very cautiously, my only thoughts on safely reaching home. Suddenly, a rabbit scurried across the three-lane highway, straight in front of my car. I couldn't help but hit it. The shock caused me to burst into tears, crying for the rabbit, for those who had died that day, and for the relief that somehow I'd been spared.

'What did it all mean?' I wondered. Three souls had left their bodies along my journey. I just wanted to get home.

I opened my car window a little to get some fresh air. "Ouch!" I cried out. A small stone had managed to find its way through the one-inch space in my window and hit me on my cheek. I wondered how this could happen since there were no cars driving by. Was it a reminder that I had eluded a terrible end?

I thought of the three unusual incidents of that day and knew some profound message was being given to me. Whenever anything happens to me in threes, I know Spirit is giving me a message.

When I finally arrived home, I reviewed my dream journal to see if I had any dreams relating to the events of the day. I found the two dreams in my journal. I felt a strong connection between the dream five years back, the dream two weeks before the accident, and what I experienced at the accident.

After reviewing my dreams, I understood that there were two roads my life could have taken. If I had chosen a different path in my life, one of service to the self, I would have left this earth on that day. But twelve years ago I had chosen to follow the path of love and to consciously serve Spirit in my life. Since then I'd followed my inner voice, always trusting and listening to the voice of my inner guide, and because of that my destiny had changed. At the end of that momentous day, I knew I had a purpose in being here. My life had been spared so that I could continue to serve in this life as a conscious being. I am forever grateful.

~ *Judy Vashti Persad*

Managing Personal Growth

When I first saw that my employer offered a class called "Managing Personal Growth," it sounded like a seminar that would help me to obtain a promotion. Advancement, economic security, stability, the American Dream – just what I wanted out of life.

However, strange things happened when the "pre-workshop test" forced me to rank my life values in order of importance. The values I ranked most important turned out to be love, family, religion, health, inner harmony and freedom. Every one of my high-ranking values was contrary to the life I lived. I had built my career and my life around avoiding time to promote these values.

Some of the values I ranked the lowest on the "test" included wealth, advancement, stability and conformity. Yet those were the areas where I spent most of my waking hours. These values were false gods, yet I worshiped them constantly.

Take love and affection, the value I ranked the highest. I spent a small fraction of my time actually practicing love and affection. I certainly loved no one at work, and my work schedule forced me to spend minimal time with the family and friends I loved.

Family ranked second on my list of values. Not only did I barely see my immediate family, I often made excuses to avoid going to any family functions. If I did show up, I left as early as possible. Life was too stressful to linger.

Religion, third on my list, was a real joke. I constantly vowed to give my life to God, yet sometimes didn't think about Him all day. Hardly ever did I feel like going to church. After all, I worked hard and deserved to sleep in late on Sunday.

Fourth on my list of values was health. I knew what I should and should not eat, drink, and smoke; yet junk food continued to dominate my life, and I never refused an offer of a glass of wine or beer. I let myself get stressed out every day, and often opted for television over exercise.

The fifth most important value on my list was inner harmony. What a fantastic concept! Somewhat foreign, though. Would I never be happy until I obtained inner harmony? It was sort of a vicious circle. If no happiness, then no inner harmony. Yet if no inner harmony, then no happiness.

Freedom was my sixth highest value, yet I had chosen a profession that chained me to a desk that I detested. Most of my "to do list" was based on someone else's ideas of what was important. Freedom to be my own boss remained a dream due to self-imposed barriers.

In addition, I found that the values I ranked lowest on the test were those that I was committed to the most. The value I ranked lowest was money, yet it was something I thought of quite often. How to make more, how to spend less, how to buy all of the things I wanted.

Advancement or promotion also ranked low on my list. Yet dreams of the boss's job and plotting how to advance took more time than dreaming of my so-called priorities.

Conformity was the final value that I ranked low. If it was so unimportant, why did I often nod in agreement when I didn't agree, or long for the material goods of someone else?

It's strange that God chose a work-related training course to finally let me see what's really important.

And it's not my job.

~ *Donna Gundle-Krieg*

A New Way Of Seeing

Our deepest wishes are whispers of our authentic selves.
We must learn to respect them.
We must learn to listen.
– Sarah Ban Breathnach

I was a single parent, living in Toronto with one son, and working full time at The Canadian National Institute for the Blind as a Social Worker. I'd always had perfect vision until one day, while sitting at my desk, I was shocked when my central vision started to blur in my left eye while I was reading a document. As the day went on, my vision worsened, so much so that before the day was over, I had an appointment with the eye doctor.

After a series of tests, the ophthalmologist could find nothing seriously wrong with me. Nevertheless, within two days I was horrified when I could see only black through my left eye. It was December 15, 1990, a day I will never forget. I shook with terror as I looked into the mirror and said out loud, "What is happening to me?"

I immediately sought advice from a dear friend and gifted psychic, Carole Matthews. "Get the tapes, *You can Heal Your Life* by Louise Hay, and listen to them every night when you go to bed for three months," she said. I remember thinking with more than just skepticism, 'My vision has gone in one eye, and I'm supposed to listen to tapes?'

With little else to do, I bought the tapes and began listening to them each night before bed. It was amazing.

Within a few days, I began to look at life in a more positive and healing way. I started paying more attention to my thoughts and to the words I chose to speak. I learned that the mind is extremely powerful and that what we think does manifest.

Prior to my vision loss, I remembered saying things like, "I don't want to 'see' this anymore," and, "I can't do this anymore." I had very negative thinking. I remember feeling stuck. I was burned out!

I wondered, 'Have I created all of this?'

'Yes,' I realized. I was responsible for my vision loss! The power of my mind astounded me. But I realized that I could manifest the power to heal myself too. Each night I would go to bed listening to audio books by Wayne Dyer, Louise Hay, and many other wonderful authors. I researched hands-on healing techniques such as Reiki and learned that placing my hands over my eyes every night could provide a healing energy. I was intrigued by self-healing and the possibilities. I soon took a Reiki course and received my degree.

My thoughts had changed, and my vision was returning gradually. Three months passed when I suddenly had an urge to draw wildlife birds! With no prior art lessons, I began to skillfully draw, first a blue heron, then an eagle, then many more wild birds. I was amazed how this urge to draw just poured through me effortlessly onto paper. I felt magical. My birds were magical. Everything I sketched became alive on paper as well as inside of me!

The more I sketched, the more my vision improved. I continued this healing process until after two years my eyesight was fully restored.

Today, I am a commissioned artist/designer living and growing on magical Salt Spring Island, British Columbia, and I am proud to be exhibiting and selling my work across the globe. I have an online company where I sell my cards and other artwork. I thank the Universe for giving me the opportunity to change how I looked at life and for showing me the power of my thoughts. The gift in losing my vision was in truly learning to see.

~ Andrea Leake

The Red Chair Experiment

Several years ago, I was invited to give a talk on the subject of manifesting abundance. As a speaker, it is one of my favorite topics, and one that I had addressed on a number of previous occasions. Wanting to approach the subject with renewed insight, it occurred to me to conduct a unique experiment where I would consciously manifest something in my life to demonstrate the principles I taught in my talk.

In doing so, I hoped to gain deeper understanding of how the manifestation process worked and the part that we play individually when we work with Spirit to bring about a desired result in our lives.

The obvious first step was to choose a subject for my experiment. It had to be something specific, something tangible, neither too big nor too small. At the time, my husband and I owned a sofa and two rather uncomfortable wrought iron chairs, which technically provided enough seating, but I longed for a more comfortable chair in which a guest could sit and feel welcome.

A new living room chair had actually been on my inner wish list for some time, but the longing had been vague instead of purposeful and exact, so I set out to make my request specific, since that is what I teach others when I talk of the manifestation process. What kind of chair? What color? Finally, after giving the matter some thought, I decided that a red chair would be best – something plush and comfortable. Yes, a red chair it was.

There was, however, one more very important stipulation that I had to place on this experiment. You see, at the time I was off on maternity leave, and our family was on a very tight budget. It simply was not the time to be buying any furniture. So the chair had to be free. Under ordinary circumstances, this might have stopped me in my tracks, convincing me of the impossibility of my request, but since it was just an experiment, I had nothing to lose. I was free to simply ask and see what might come.

With my chair in mind, I closed my eyes, filled myself with a feeling of gratitude for all the blessings in my life, and quietly sang a sacred word HU (pronounced "hue"), a nondirected prayer that has the power to open the heart to Divine Love and the blessings of life. Then I silently sent my request out into the ether.

Perhaps because this was not a pressingly urgent matter, it was relatively easy to achieve the state of detached acceptance and openness that is necessary for manifestation. In fact, I felt confident in saying that the chair was, at that very minute, already on its way to me. I reminded myself that it was not my job to know exactly where it would come from or even when it would arrive. All I had to do was to trust completely that it was on its way and that Spirit would orchestrate its arrival in a way that was best for both me and anyone else involved. Having done my part, I went to bed.

The next morning, I took my ten-month-old son out for a walk at a brisk pace, pushing the stroller in front of me. Along the way I passed all the familiar neighborhood stores and restaurants and a nearby retirement home, in front of which I noticed a parked moving van. It struck me that I had never before seen a moving van there, though surely people must move in on occasion. At any rate, I kept walking until my son fell asleep. Then I slowly turned back and headed for home, my pace now slower in order to extend his nap.

As I passed the retirement home I saw the moving van was still parked, and noticed that various pieces of furniture had been moved out onto the concrete walkway in front of the building. Amongst the other items, I spotted a red chair.

I smiled to myself, knowing this was a sure sign that my chair was on its way. "Yes," I thought to myself, "a red chair just like that would be perfect."

As I passed the chair, a glint caught my eye, and I turned around to take another look. There appeared to be some sort of shiny strip across one of its arms. I was about to ignore it and walk away, but an inner whispering urged me towards it. As I moved closer, I gasped, for there on the arm of the chair was a strip of wide tape on which had been written, "Goodwill." I felt a rush of cold excitement race through my body. Surely they were not getting rid of this beautiful chair! I walked around it and saw no holes, no damage at all. Could it be that easy? I knew I had to at least ask, so I waited until one of the moving men came out of the building and inquired about the chair. He confirmed that it was supposed to go to Goodwill, a local organization that recycles used items to raise money for disadvantaged people, and offered to ask the woman he was working for about it. Excitedly I waited, pushing the stroller in circles to keep my slumbering son asleep.

About five minutes later, a woman came out of the building. She smiled and explained that she was helping her in-laws move into the retirement residence. They now realized that the tiny apartment wouldn't hold all of their furniture, so the chair and a few other items were slated to go to Goodwill. She went on to tell me that the chair had been in a seldom-used room of her in-laws' house and therefore, despite being vintage, had rarely been used. When I offered to pay her, she refused, saying that if I could take it away within the next fifteen minutes, it was mine for free, since they had to clear the walkway within that time, and it would save them from having to deliver the chair to Goodwill.

I stood there stunned and grateful, and shared with her my experiment to manifest a red chair the previous evening. As I finished my story, the two of us shared a moment of wonder at the extraordinary events that had unfolded.

Darlene Montgomery

My husband, who is an actor, had left earlier for an audition, taking our car. Nonetheless, I tried to reach him on his cell phone and was surprised when he answered and told me he had finished the audition early and was already home. All of this meant that within minutes he was there, pulling up in front of the retirement residence and staring with disbelief at the gorgeous chair that was now ours. I thanked the woman one last time as my husband loaded the chair into the car and drove off, and then I continued home slowly on foot, my still-slumbering son in the stroller, and my mind simply jumping with excitement.

The experiment was concluded in less than twenty-four hours! Even I was amazed. That night I was filled with awe and gratitude for the gift I'd received. I now had a living example of the power of manifestation to share for my talk on abundance.

And if I ever need a reminder of how abundance is everywhere and available for those who can open to receive, there's a lovely plush red chair sitting in my living room to prove it.

~ *Shelley Hyndman*

Magical Love Story

The people we are in relationship with are always
a mirror, reflecting our own beliefs, and
simultaneously we are mirrors, reflecting their
beliefs. So ... relationship is one of the most powerful tools for growth ... . If we look honestly at our
relationships, we can see so much about
how we have created them.
– Shakti Gawain

At the time my story began, I was living in Montreal and had been single for four years. I was really ready to meet someone. When I mentioned my desire to a colleague at work, she suggested writing letters to the unknown friend I would like to meet. I took her advice and bought a notebook where I began writing letters to my dear friend, telling him how I felt about him and how wonderful it was to have finally met the love of my life. Each day I wrote a new letter. I also took the time to create a written list describing the qualities of my ideal mate.

Somehow doing this exercise connected me with an intense desire while bringing me in touch with the uncon-scious fears that had been holding me back from letting a romance happen.

While walking to work each morning, I repeatedly programmed my mind to attract my friend, convincing myself that he existed somewhere, and that he was waiting

Darlene Montgomery

158

for me. I wrote thirty-three of these letters over a period of four months, and then I just surrendered to God.

In October 2001, I joined a business networking group through which I met many different people from all backgrounds, faiths, and professions. My main language is French, so speaking in English forced me to overcome one of my fears. One of the members, Bruce, told me about a personal growth seminar to be held in Montreal at the end of May 2002. It sounded very interesting, and I decided to attend. He sent me all the details and called me back for a pre-seminar session.

For the last ten years I had been writing down my dreams in a journal. The day before his call, I reviewed my dream entries for that month and in one of my recent dreams, I saw myself alone with a group of men, all gathered for a special meeting. They were wearing jeans and casual clothes, and most had grey hair and appeared to be about forty-five to fifty years old. These men seemed to be linked together in a strong bond, but the dream didn't show how. When Bruce mentioned I would be the only woman in the group for this upcoming session, I felt that the dream was somehow connected. I knew that the dream held a message for me and that I had to go to the meeting to get it.

When I arrived at the meeting, there were eight men, most with gray hair, wearing jeans and hugging each other. I knew I was in the right place. They shared with me very personal experiences, and throughout the evening I felt close to them in an unexpected way. As I didn't have all the money to attend this seminar, three of them offered to give me money in advance to help out. I was so touched by their generosity that tears came to my eyes.

When asked to fill out a form about the purpose for being at the seminar, I wrote spontaneously that I wanted to be engaged in a relationship. The week prior to the seminar, I asked myself, 'What can I bring to this seminar? What will

I receive from the seminar?' Nothing happened until the night before, when I had three dreams.

The first dream was about practical details involved in the weekend. In the second dream, I saw myself standing by a man, feeling very safe and secure with my head on his shoulder. In the third dream, I searched for the name of a street in a very dark place and was unable to find it. Then I saw a store with a light. I entered and an old woman came to me. She was bent with something that looked like a piece of wood in her lower back. I asked what was going on with her. She answered that she had worked very hard, and this was the consequence.

I woke up, wrote my dreams, and then prepared myself to leave for the seminar. As I entered the room, I was immediately attracted by the eyes of a man sitting at the registration table at the main entrance. I felt that he was a very sensitive person, a little bit shy and fragile. He gave me my nametag, and I went upstairs.

I was chatting with Bruce when I first saw the man at the table stand up; to my surprise he had the same posture as the old woman in my dream. When I asked Bruce about him, he told me his name was Marvin from Ottawa.

I just stood up, walked over to him, and said, "I don't know what we have to share during this weekend, but I would like to speak with you. I saw you in my dreams, and I trust my dreams." He looked at me somewhat startled and didn't say anything, so I went to take my seat. During the day he stared at me several times, and we spoke a little during the breaks. At one point I asked Marvin about his back, and he told me how at the age of thirteen, he had had a surgery for scoliosis. As he'd grown, his fused spine made it impossible for him to stand straight.

Later that evening when the seminar ended, Marvin offered me a lift home. During the drive home we became more acquainted, and when we arrived at my house, I kissed him on each cheek, and we said goodbye. I was full of a strange energy, as if there were no limits and everything was possible.

Before going to sleep, I asked to have a dream to show me if Marvin was the man I'd been looking for, but my excitement made it impossible for me to sleep that night. The next morning Marvin picked me up to drive me to the second day of the seminar. It was a very windy and cold day, and he said that he hadn't slept very well. During the seminar, we had a very emotional exchange where people were able to move freely in the room after having listened to testimonials written or spoken by close friends or parents. Marvin and I connected again during that time, and I could see that we fit so well together.

Marvin shared with me his purpose statement, which said that he would like to be engaged in a relationship for the rest of his life. Our timing, it seemed, was perfect. The seminar both enabled me to connect to a state of unconditional love and prepared me to receive the great gift of love for which I'd asked. Marvin and I married exactly one year later, in June 2003. Since then, our love has continued to grow. I moved to Ottawa with Marvin, and I'm gathering clients for my new practice in acupuncture.

By believing in my dreams and the power of love, I found my true love. I hope our story will inspire you to believe that anything is possible.

~Claudette Viau

Santa Fe Dreamin'

When the Soul wishes to experience something,
she throws an image of the experience out before her
and enters into her own image.
— Meister Eckhart

This story began with a dream:

In it, I arrive in Santa Fe, New Mexico. In the background, Joni Mitchell sings, "Do You Know the Way to Santa Fe?" (Okay, I know it's Dionne Warwick and "San Jose," but this is a dream.) In front of me, multi-colored animated flowers bob side to side to the beat of the music. I pass them and walk on into the center of town. There, I'm drawn to a store selling suede clothing and accessories handmade in pastel shades of every color of the rainbow. I enter and meet the artisan, a striking woman with a powerful, almost otherworldly presence. As we talk, we both feel like we've known each other all our lives. I tell her I'm visiting from New York, where I live.

She looks right at me and says, "You should move to Santa Fe." She explains that she used to live in New York City, too, and learned a lot there. But it was in Santa Fe that she was able to manifest out into the world everything she'd learned in that city. "And you could, too," she says. "At least move here for part of the year." I consider what she is saying and decide it's true. I should move.

When I woke up in my apartment in New York City, my heart was pounding. I was unable to shake the feeling that this was more than a dream. No dream of mine had ever been this vivid, nor had one ever so blatantly told me what to do. I had never even been to Santa Fe or thought of visiting, let alone moving there. Besides, my life was in New York – my work, my friends, my relationship, my family, the culture and diversity that I loved. The thought of leaving had never occurred to me. But somehow that dream wouldn't go away.

In the coming months, it would flash through my mind over and over again. And, suddenly, Santa Fe was all the rage. There were articles on Santa Fe in all the magazines. Even Bloomingdale's had a series of window displays featuring the "Santa Fe look." It became a regular topic of conversation between my partner and me, so much so that once when he was traveling, he bought a Santa Fe Railroad hat for me and a red and black Santa Fe railroad bandanna for my German Shepherd to wear around his neck. But we never actually thought of moving there.

Fast forward two years. My partner and I had broken up. My freelance work had dried up. Many of my friends had moved away, or we'd moved in different directions. I couldn't even continue to live in my apartment because my dog had developed a degenerative back condition and could no longer climb the four flights of stairs to get to it.

It was time to move, and Santa Fe kept coming up into my consciousness, even though I didn't really want it there. Maybe I'd move after the first of the year, I thought to myself. Try it for three months. If I liked it, I'd stay. If not, I'd move to San Francisco. It was August at the time. But I had the strongest feeling that I needed to go right away, not wait. And even though I usually did not act on feelings quickly like that, this time I did. I sold most of my belongings, stored or shipped the rest, and in mid-September, my German Shepherd and I boarded a plane for New Mexico.

I had still never visited there. I only knew the name of a waiter my friend had become acquainted with when she'd traveled through Santa Fe the previous spring.

When I arrived, I was awed by New Mexico's expansive landscape and the open sky after living so long amongst the caverns of New York's skyscrapers and high rises. But although I appreciated its great beauty, I also experienced an undercurrent of darkness. I had an immediate and inexplicable dislike for the place. *What have I done?* I asked myself. Regardless, I started looking for a place to live. I also called my friend's acquaintance, who kindly invited me to stay with him and his sister until the weekend, when his own family was coming to visit.

In the process of house hunting, I connected with a woman whose friends were planning to leave town for three months and probably needed a house sitter. "I'll know some time this week," she said. "Why don't you call me every couple days and check in? It sounds perfect for you."

After two calls with no news, she told me about a house for rent that she'd just heard about. "It's out in the middle of the desert and has incredible views of both mountain ranges. Your dog will have lots of space. It's so amazing that if you see it, you'll probably never want to leave Santa Fe."

I had to at least see this place, so I called and made an appointment. The owner of the house, Jonah Blue, warmly invited me inside for a tour. He had white hair that glowed like an angel's. It had turned prematurely when he was in his mid 30's, he would tell me later. Of medium height and build, he was dressed in blue jeans and an orange shirt, and he wore a silver ring shaped like an eagle.

His living room was filled with memorabilia from the Wizard of Oz – one of my favorite movies – hanging plates, posters and a large painting of Emerald City. Oddly enough, I was wearing red leather sneakers that day, my own ruby slippers. I definitely felt like I was on a journey down the Yellow Brick Road.

I asked him about the movie as he showed me the house. As an adult, he'd had a profound experience watching it, he told me. "I realized I had been like the Wizard, hiding behind the curtain all my life. Since then, it's been my job to come out and show my authentic self."

We talked easily and freely with each other. He was leaving Santa Fe, after two years of living there, he said, because nothing had gone quite right. His relationship had broken up. While he'd always connected easily with people, he hadn't been able to make friends. He hadn't even been able to sell his house after it had been on the market for several months. He'd finally rented it. Then, the night before, the rental had fallen through. In five days, he was moving back to Marin County, just outside San Francisco, where he had lived once before. Jonah had called everyone he'd ever met in Santa Fe hoping to find another renter. My housesitting contact had been one of those people.

The house was indeed fabulous, but I didn't know if I wanted to take on a lease and live so far out of town. I told him I'd like to consider it over the weekend. Meanwhile, I was taking off to explore Taos, because I could no longer stay with my friend's acquaintances.

"Well, if that's the reason you're going to Taos, you and your German Shepherd are welcome to stay here until I leave," Jonah said. "Take one of the back bedrooms. No strings attached. I'd welcome the companionship – and you could find out if you'd enjoy living this far out of town."

Surprised by the generous offer, I was even more surprised by my response. "OK, thanks. I'd love to," I heard myself say. *Are you nuts?* My rational mind countered. *What if he's a psychotic killer?* But it was my intuition and heart that had been leading this Santa Fe journey thus far, not reason, and it reassured me. *He seems friendly*, it said. *He's into the Wizard of Oz., and he's a writer, like you. Besides, you have a large German Shepherd.* That voice won out.

For the next two days, when Jonah wasn't busy packing, we were talking non-stop about our lives. We found out that both our partners had dumped us on exactly the same day nine months earlier – two days after Thanksgiving. It was a day indelibly marked in our memories because of the vast holiday season that lay ahead.

One of our favorite topics was spirituality. I had begun exploring mine the last two years I'd lived in New York, but had had no one to talk to about it. Without being drawn to any particular religion or teacher, I'd been at a loss to put into words what "being spiritual" or "having faith" meant to me. In two days of talking to Jonah, I became clear that I was creating my own spiritual path, and that for me, following the call of my dream, no matter where it led me, had been part of that. I felt myself coming home to myself, in a way I never had before – like Dorothy in Oz.

Jonah took a similar approach to spirituality, taking bits and pieces from many traditions. He was creating a personalized path which recognized and honored the divine within each human being and all other life forms, too.

That weekend, Jonah and I began to have strong feelings for each other – something neither of us had anticipated. Jonah was leaving town to begin anew. And for the first time in my life, I was truly happy being single. I wanted to spend time writing in Santa Fe, getting to know myself better – not getting involved with someone. Especially a someone who'd be gone soon. I envisioned myself left behind, this puddle of devastated mush, trying to pick myself up again and get on with my new life. No, romance was not on my agenda.

We discussed what was happening and decided to consciously shut down any romantic feelings that were emerging. Then we spent the rest of our time together simply enjoying each other's friendship. We explored art galleries, talked about spiritual teachers and practices – Ramana Maharshi, the Course in Miracles, meditation, spirit guides. We watched old movies on TV and discovered a shared love for film.

He told me about Marin County, where he was moving. I realized that Marin County sounded much more like a place I wanted to live than Santa Fe: lots of nature, the ocean,

access to a big city, on the cutting edge spiritually and cultur-
ally. The day Jonah left, he told me to give him a call if I
decided to come to San Francisco after my three months
were up in Santa Fe. "You can stay with me until you find a
place," he said. And then he was gone.

Strangely, as soon as Jonah pulled away in his car, whatever draw I'd felt to being in Santa Fe was gone, too. And I
couldn't find anything to grab onto. The housesitting job fell
through. Having decided not to rent Jonah's house, I could-
n't find another place to live. For two weeks, I went through
the motions. But my heart wasn't in it. It was already in
Marin.

Now, just as strongly as I'd originally felt the urge to go to
Santa Fe, I kept hearing over and over again, *You're done. Go
to Marin. Don't wait for three months.*

Why not go? I thought to myself. Besides, now I had a
friend there, too – Jonah. This "following my inner guidance"
and taking leaps of faith was sure becoming a fast habit.

One month after I moved to Santa Fe, I flew on to San
Francisco instead. Outside the airplane window, the sky was a
deep blue. The ocean shimmered against the rolling hills and
cliffs on its edge. A joy welled up from the deepest part of me.
"This is my home now. I'm moving here right now," I told the
man sitting next to me. My journey to find my next place was
complete. My new life was starting.

I did stay with Jonah. And, within the first week, I found
a place I could move into one week later. Only I never moved
in. Jonah and I realized we were in love, and neither one of us
wanted me to go to my new apartment. Five months later, we
were married at a friend's house overlooking San Francisco
Bay. We wrote our own vows and included a quote from Ram
Dass, a spiritual teacher, in our ceremony. He talked about
the importance of having a conscious marriage whose ultimate purpose was found in going to God together. We didn't
know then how that journey would include many tests and
trials in addition to the love we celebrated. But always, since

that fated meeting in Santa Fe, we've faced them together. In February 2005, we celebrated our 21st anniversary.

But that's not all. There's one more piece to this story that involves that Santa Fe dream. Ten years after meeting, Jonah and I had moved to Southern Oregon. There, at a party, we met Suzanna Solomon, a spiritual counselor and artist, who taught people to connect to their divine guidance. We found out that she had lived in Santa Fe when Jonah did. Then he remembered that he'd done a session with her to connect with his first spirit guide shortly before meeting me. In fact, when we toured galleries there, he bought a small painting on wood that reminded him of that guide.

At the time, Suzanna had just begun her spiritual counseling. Before that, she'd worked in Santa Fe hand-making and selling suede accessories and clothing, done in pastel shades of every color in the rainbow.

Something about her was weirdly familiar. Looking at her more closely, my heart began to pound. Suzanna was the craftswoman from my original Santa Fe dream, the one who'd told me to move to Santa Fe. Now she had come in human form – just when we expressly needed to connect more deeply to our own inner divine guidance and wisdom to help us with the challenges we were facing. Suzanna became our spiritual mentor and remains our beloved friend today.

Once, many years ago, I had a dream which called on me to take a leap of faith. For a while I didn't recognize the call. But that Santa Fe dream took on a life of its own. It lived concurrently beside my own life until I was ready to trust its message.

Later, following that call – reluctantly at first – meant giving up what I knew and taking a risk with the unknown. It meant staying the course even though I couldn't control the outcome or the unexpected detours and inconveniences that presented themselves. I was forever changed.

Just think of what I would have missed if I hadn't followed that call. I would have had another life, for sure. But it would not have been this one, the life I was called to by a dream.

~ *Alissa M. Lukara*

About the Author

Darlene Montgomery is a writer, editor, and respected authority on dreams who speaks to groups and organizations on uplifting subjects. Her first book, *Dream Yourself Awake*, was published in November, 1999. It chronicles the journey she took to discover her own divine mission using sleeping dreams, waking dreams, and intuition. Her second book, *Conscious Women – Conscious Lives: Powerful and Transformational Stories of Healing Body, Mind, and Soul,* released March 2004, quickly became a best seller.

As a consultant, Darlene has also helped compile two of the famous *Chicken Soup* books. Her stories have appeared in *Chicken Soup for the Parent's Soul* and *Chicken Soup for the Canadian Soul, Vitality Magazine, Synchronicity Magazine,* and the WTN website. Darlene's recent book media campaign took her across Canada and the U.S., where she appeared on national television and radio shows, including Michael Coren Live, Rogers Daytime, ON TV news, Breakfast Television, The Patty Purcell Show, The Life Station, and more. Darlene also operates her own public relations firm, helping to promote authors and experts.

For more on Darlene and her work visit:
www.lifedreams.org.

Other books by Darlene Montgomery

Dream Yourself Awake

This autobiography reads like a spiritual mystery. A question asked of the author by a mysterious guide sets the author on a journey to uncover the source of her deep spiritual illness, leading her to discover the one deep truth that needs to be understood for her to be healed. Throughout the story, hundreds of personal dreams act as clues to solve the mystery, leading to the personal revelation of the author.

Dreams are a natural homing device residing in the heart of soul. Many of us are aware of a yearning or sense of destiny, purpose or mission we must find before our life is complete. In *Dream Yourself Awake*, Darlene Montgomery tells the story behind the search for her own mission in a series of dreams, waking dream and inner experiences. As we share her journey, we will discover how to use these same tools to see beyond the illusions of the mind, and travel straight to the heart of our divine purpose.

To order your copy email Darlene:
lifedreams@idirect.com

First in the Series,

Conscious Women –
Conscious Lives:
Powerful & Transformational
Stories of Healing Body Mind
& Soul

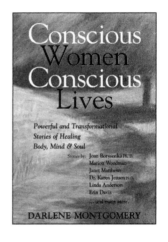

In this extraordinary collection
of personal revelation, women
share their deepest and heartfelt experiences of healing from
loss, illness and accident. These
stories show how the journey of
facing some of life's greatest obstacles can be followed by a
joyous emergence from the darkness of despair, and a return
to the light of life, love and new wisdom.

These true stories by women, for women, help open the
heart, heal the spirit, and bring peace of mind during some of
life's most challenging times. As each author brings a treasure
from her own rich experience, she contributes to the pool of
wisdom we share on this planet of how each of us can meet
our greatest fears to rise again with wisdom, grace and
courage.

Whatever challenges you presently face, these stories
offer hope, reassurance, comfort and proud examples of the
resilient nature and wisdom of women.

ISBN 0-9734186-1-3   216 pages PB   US $13.95   Cdn $19.95

A Message from the Publisher

In keeping with White Knight Publication's mandate to bring great titles of social concern to book and library shelves across North America, I am indeed fortunate as publisher to have been able to be closely involved with this latest publication in White Knight's "Remarkable Women Series".

Conscious Women – Conscious Lives Book Two lives up to expectations that women across North America constantly provide the nurturing component that continues to make our countries so great. These stories from across Canada and the United States of America, bring home those concerns that women have for other women providing love, nourishment and hope for our present and future generations.

Remarkable women, everyone. Thank you!

Contributors

Kati Alexandra is just underway with a 'new life' on her own, and she chooses to live it with joy. Her time is devoted to her love of writing, inscribed on rocks and in artistic expressions while she is creating her own book. It is her greatest desire to inspire others to find their own magnificence. This is the focus of her coaching, playshops, seminars, and conversation circles. Giving back to children through the empowerment of those who work with them is her vision. The joyful celebration of life at its fullest is her goal as she creates programs and rituals honoring the unlimited possibilities that her own new life is offering her. She offers a unique blend of many years of consciousness training added to her thirty years of experience as a classroom teacher. She shares her numerous gifts through Reiki healing sessions, guided creative visualization manifestations, yoga therapy, coaching as an 'Essentials for the Best Year of Your Life' coach, journaling, and dancing the joy in your heart playshops. She readily creates workshops to suit individual group focuses. All her work is based on the belief that we have all the answers within us as we connect to our inner wisdom. Kati invites contact through email at *katioutwest@aol.com*. She can also be reached at her Vancouver residence at 604-736-7973.

Tracy Clausell-Alexander resides in Southern California with her husband and five children. She is a financial analyst who possesses a love for writing, using her personal experiences to influence her literary works. Tracy's stories have been published in *Chicken Soup for the African American Soul*.

Everything that she writes is dedicated to the memory of her parents and her little boy, Eric. Please contact her at: *tdclausell@comcast.net*

Barbara Allport is a therapist in private practice in Toronto and Bancroft, Ontario, Canada. She resides in Bancroft with her two cats. She can be reached at b*arballport@fcicanada.net*.

Marianne Bai-Woo is the former publisher and editor of BLOOM Magazine – Women Growing in Life, a self-published magazine dedicated to inspiring and informing women to create a life that is as unique as they are. She has ten years of fashion and visual merchandising experience and fifteen years in the marketing, publishing, graphics, and printing. Presently she is a creative consultant inspiring people to live the life of their dreams, through her company The Creative Eye and BLOOM Promotions. She is an avid writer, artist, photographer, and insatiable reader of all material that is provocative, intriguing, and fun. She lives in Unionville, Ontario, with her two greatest inspirations and teachers, sons Taylor, 10, and Connor, 3; and her husband Steve, who has taught her what unconditional love truly is. Marianne can be reached at *marianne@bloompromotions.com* / 416-564-7077.

Sybil Barbour resides in Kitchener, Ontario with her husband and an aged cat. She is a retired registered nurse and midwife. She's recently fulfilled a lifelong dream of traveling to Italy, Greece, Scotland, and New Zealand. You can contact her at *sybilbarbour@sympatico.ca*.

Cynthia Brian is the NY Times best-selling co-author of *Chicken Soup for the Gardener's Soul*, author of *Be the Star You Are!*®, *99 Gifts for Living, Loving, Laughing, and Learning to Make a Difference*, *The Business of Show Business*, and *Miracle Moments*®. She is an internationally acclaimed keynote speaker, personal growth consultant, host of radio and TV shows, syndicated columnist, and acting coach.

Often referred to by the media as "the Renaissance woman with soul," Cynthia has over two decades of experience working in the entertainment field as an actor, producer, writer, coach, designer, and casting director. She is the Founder/CEO of the 501 (c)(3) charity, Be the Star You Are! Her motto is "To be a leader, you must be a reader!" Cynthia is dedicated to helping others achieve their dreams by implementing their unique gifts, and she has coached many aspiring thespians, writers, and professionals to fame and fortune. Tune into her weekly radio program, Be the Star You Are! on WORLDTALK radio, or contact her for coaching or speaking at: Cynthia Brian, Starstyle® Productions, LLC, PO Box 422, Moraga, CA, USA 94556, 925-377-STAR (7827) *www.star-style.com* / *www.starstyleproductions.com* *www.bethestaryouare.org*

Merrily Bronson died at home on January 18, 1995, surrounded by her family. She will be remembered for her integrity, her spirituality, and her unconditional acceptance of those around her. Merrily and her husband Jim enjoyed a deep and growing relationship over the 25 years of their marriage. In addition to being a Marriage, Family and Child Counselor, Merrily was a faithful friend to many and a wonderful mother who raised two remarkable sons. She gave all who knew her a strong sense of respect and approval and brought people together, bringing out the best in them. She was much loved by all who knew her.

In 1990 Merrily and Jim founded the Challenge Learning Center, a nonprofit agency that provided programs for people facing life-threatening illnesses and outdoor programs for at-risk youth, families, and communities. A gifted writer, Merrily made memorable contributions to the BCA newsletter with articles on "Cancer as a Turning Point," "Healing Journeys," and "The HER2/neu Monoclonal Antibody." She is deeply missed.

Dr. Georgina Cannon is recognized by many in the media as "The Source" for expert opinion in the field of hypnotherapy and issues around complementary wellness treatments. She is a certified master clinical hypnotherapist, a vibrant international lecturer, teacher, and director of a hypnosis school and clinic. For more on Georgina Cannon, visit www.ont-hypnosis-centre.com.

Deborah Davis is an active member of the Ottawa Police Service. An accomplished singer, she is a member of the Ottawa Police Choir and the Temple of ECK Choir. She is a Reiki Master, and she continues to study energy medicine and alternative healing. She hopes to start a second career in Transformational Healing.

Erin Davis was born in Edmonton, Alberta and as a result of her father's Air Force career, was raised in many places, including Ottawa, Trenton, and Britain. Erin's introduction to show business came at an early age when she sang regularly with her grandfather's orchestra. Her love of performing led her to study Radio Broadcasting at Loyalist College in Belleville. By her second year, she was hosting an afternoon radio show on CIGL-FM.

Upon graduation on the Dean's List, Erin moved to Windsor, Ontario and began reading morning news on CKLW, The Big Eight. Shortly after, she became the first female morning co-host in the powerful Detroit market. A station format change led Erin to move to Toronto, where she co-hosted the morning show on All News Radio CKO for four years. Her big break came in the summer of 1988 when the call came for her to do morning news on the popular Daynard Drive-In on 98.1 CHFI. The chemistry between Erin and host Don Daynard was magical, and she soon became Don's co-host, a partnership that became hugely popular over their eleven years together until Don's retirement. Erin continued to host the CHFI morning show until the spring of 2003.

Following a number of guest-host positions at CFTO and Global, Erin wrote and performed a nightly commentary on CFTO News in 1998 and 1999 called *Just So You Know*. Then, for two seasons, she hosted a nightly talk show (more than 200 episodes) on Rogers Television called *The Erin Davis Show*. This lifestyle and wellness program, which was seen in over two million homes in Southern Ontario, received an award in its second season as Canada's best cable talk show. In 2002, Erin was honored by being named the year's first *Chatelaine* Woman Of Influence, joining the ranks of such luminaries as Former Prime Minister Kim Campbell, Indigo chief Heather Reisman, Astronaut Roberta Bondar, and fellow broadcaster Pamela Wallin. Erin writes a daily internet journal that is available at www.erindavis.com.

Ruth Edgett accumulated more than 20 years experience as a journalist and communicator before turning to the pursuit of her true loves: being with horses and writing for pleasure. Ruth's previous careers have included newspaper reporting and consulting in environmental communications. She is a former President of the Hamilton, Ontario, chapter of the Canadian Public Relations Society. She has an MS in Public Communications from Syracuse University and a BA in Philosophy from the University of Prince Edward Island. Ruth lives with her husband in Ancaster, Ontario, and is pleased to be owned by a cat, Gizmo, and a horse, Maggie.

Cathleen Fillmore owns and operates Speakers Gold, the proactive Speakers Bureau that coaches people on getting into the paid speaking market as well as coaching speakers on how to reach the next level in their careers. She is founder and past-President of the Halifax branch of the Canadian Association of Professional Speakers, and she is a certified professional consultant with the American League of Consultants. Her upcoming book is called *The Six-Figure Income Speaker*. Cathleen is co-author of *Going for Gold: A Complete Marketing Strategy for Speakers*, and *Against All Odds: Ordi-*

nary People in Extraordinary Circumstances, both published by Elias Press, as well as *The Life of a Loyalist: Tales of Old Nova Scotia*, published by Altitude Press. To book a speaker or to talk with Cathleen about your speaking career, call 416-532-9886.

Arlene Forbes is a registered nurse. She combines twenty-four years of experience in multiple areas of nursing with her spiritual studies and her creativity as an interpretive dancer of music and poetry to create healing environments for her clients, as well as large audiences worldwide. She is an aspiring writer of fiction and inspirational stories. She lives in Minneapolis, Minnesota, with her husband, Aubrey. You can reach Arlene at *eagleforbes@qwest.net.*

Shelley Hyndman is a dynamic speaker, workshop facilitator and inspiring life coach, who has motivated thousands of individuals, across North America and Europe, to transform their lives and move closer to their dreams. For 15 years, she has presented talks and workshops to entrepreneurs, women, youth, writers and artists, as well as at spiritual conferences both in North America and abroad.

With her uniquely inspiring and uplifting style, and a talent for conveying esoteric truths and universal principles in a clear, simple and down-to-earth manner, Shelley focuses on exploring the ways in which we can work with Spirit and life to fulfill our greatest potential and manifest greater prosperity, joy and spiritual freedom in our lives.

It is this passion for inspiring others that also marks Shelley's work as an editor and literary coach. As the visionary founder of a unique company, The Literary Midwife, she has designed a number of exceptional programs that help aspiring and professional writers alike to literally "birth" their books, screenplays and other writing projects.

Shelley has appeared on television and has been featured in live radio and newspaper interviews. Her talk, "Higher Earning: Key Spiritual Principles to Manifesting Abundance" was presented to a group of 80 entrepreneurs and has since been published in audiocassette format.

Shelley currently lives in Toronto with her husband and two children, and continues to deliver talks and workshops on a wide range of topics, including her highly popular "Cultivating Miracles" workshop. Contact Shelley at: *www.the literarymidwife.com* or e-mail *sdrayton@theliterarymidwife.com*.

Sandra Irvine is currently living in Barrie, Ontario, working as a registered nurse in the community. Her work involves caring for many palliative patients, and she is interested in branching out into alternative therapies. She is physically active, involved in many sports and activities, including yoga. Her interests include studying reflexology, and she is currently working on obtaining her Level 2 Reiki certification. She has an avid interest in studying dreams, angels, spirituality, and past lives. To contact Sandra, send email to *butterfly961@msn.com*.

Susan Jeffers, Ph.D. is considered one of the top self-help authors in the world. Her books have been published in over 100 countries and translated into at least 30 different languages. *Feel the Fear and Do It, Anyway* launched her career as a best-selling author. Some of her many other titles include *The Feel the Fear Guide to Lasting Love, Life is Huge!, End the Struggle and Dance With Life, Opening Our Hearts to Men, and Embracing Uncertainty*. She is also a well-known public speaker and media personality. Her popular web site is *www.susanjeffers.com*.

Sheri Kaplan is the Executive Director for The Center for Positive Connections (TCPC) and a nationally recognized expert on HIV/AIDS issues, non-profit management, community outreach, and prevention education. She is a popular public speaker, having participated in over 104 speaking engagements locally to a cumulative audience of 25,000. Nationally, she has appeared in many articles in local newspapers (*Miami Herald, Sun Sentinel,* and *Street Weekly*). She has also appeared on the Discovery Channel (Berman & Berman), the Arts & Entertainment Channel (Bill Kurtis' Investigative Reports), America's Health Network (Ask the Doctor), and the Montel Williams Show (Single Women & AIDS). She recently presented a poster abstract at the International AIDS conference in Thailand titled "Surviving and Thriving with an HIV Diagnosis." TCPC also has been recognized in the *Miami New Times* newspaper (5/15/02) as providing "Best Care for HIV/AIDS-isolation." Sheri was nominated in December 2004 for the Concern Awards with the Health Foundation of South Florida. For more about Sheri, visit *www.positiveconnections.org*

Donna Gundle-Krieg lives in Milford, Michigan, and has written for several publications. She recently published a children's book called *From Desert to Detroit.* This book is about an Iraqi family who comes to America and the big city problems they face, including prejudice. The purpose of the book is to educate children and others about the complex international issues of our time. For more information, go to *www.blitzkriegpublishing.com*

Andrea Leak is a commissioned wildlife artist and a private health care facilitator. Although born and raised in the heart of Toronto, Andrea found herself desiring and dreaming of an alternative life style. She has lived and worked on magical Salt Spring Island, British Columbia, since 1997. Andrea's expression of her love for nature and the environment came to her through a gift she discovered after completing her Reiki degree in 1996. Andrea's wildlife sketches are exhibited across the globe. Her most recent creation is a line of wellness products that can be used and enjoyed by many in all walks of life. For more about Andrea and her work, visit www.koolerbandana.com or contact her at *andrea@koolerbandana.com*

Jo Leonard has presented talks and workshops for over twenty years throughout the United States and in Mexico, Canada, Australia, New Zealand, Europe, and West Africa. Her first two novel-length works of fiction are currently making the rounds of publishers, as are numerous short stories. In addition to speaking and writing, she serves as the Vice President of a commercial printing company. Jo lives in Occoquan, Virginia, a historic village 15 miles south of Washington D.C., with much-loved husband Jerry and two Siamese cats. She may be contacted at *jlionhart@aol.com*.

Alissa Lukara is president of Life Challenges, www.lifechallenges.org, a nonprofit website, whose inspirational articles and self-help tools help individuals in some 78 countries worldwide find the larger perspective and personal growth available in adversity. She is the author of *Riding the Grace: A Journey of Acceptance, Healing and Miracles*, a story of the grace that can result from accepting the unacceptable. Her articles on interpersonal relationships and communication have appeared in numerous publications. She is also a spiritual counselor and workshop leader who focuses on empowering people to discover their unique healing paths and the wholeness that lives within them – regardless of illness and adversity. Mostly, however, she considers herself a life artist, co-creating with The Great Mystery the various ups, downs, ins and outs of her glorious, beloved life. Sometimes, she even reaches that place where she can let go of all the doing and labeling stuff, and then, she simply is. Contact Alissa at *alissal@lifechallenges.org* or visit her website: *www.lifechallenges.org*.

Brenda Mallory is a legally blind artist, author, motivational speaker, journalist and comic. She taught grade one for many years in British Columbia. She lives on a five-acre bird sanctuary where she pursues her many careers. Please reach her at 250-846-5095 or at Box 550, Telkwa, British Columbia V0J 2X0.

Carole Matthews touches the lives of people everywhere with a warm heart and a keen sense of meaning and purpose. Whether given in a private session or broadcast to thousands over national media, Carole's message is one of hope, clarity, and spiritual enlightenment. Carole's inner strength and witty sense of humor comes from her own life: her roots in both Winnipeg and Keswick, Ontario, the challenge of two near-fatal car accidents, and the joys of her three children, six grandchildren, and her Bichon dog/friend Tuffy. As an intuitive medium, Carole does not speak for people; rather, she opens the door to let the communication between loved ones flow. Carole unlocks the barriers that may prevent people from realizing their potential over personal, career, health and spiritual challenges. Strength, passion, affirmation – these are some of the many gifts Carole leaves with her audience. Many have contacted Carole afterwards – sometimes years later – to recount how her message was a catalyst in changing their lives. Carole also reaches people though her Inner Voice and Guardian Angel workshops and the very popular Interactive Evening events. Her popular weekly radio/online show "The Messengerfiles" on 560 CFOS is one of Carole's many passions. Newspaper and magazine columns also are a vehicle for Carole to do what she calls "getting the much-needed message out there." For more about Carole visit *www.carolematthewsintuitive.com*.

Mary Carroll Moore has been a published writer since 1977. Her essays, articles, columns, and stories have been in over 200 publications, including *American Artist, Health, Prevention*, the *Boston Globe, Los Angeles Times*, and many other national media. Mary writes a bimonthly food column for the *Los Angeles Times* syndicate, which appears in over 86 newspapers nationwide, and a bimonthly column for the *Minneapolis Star-Tribune*. Ten of her nonfiction books are published, and she just finished her first fiction book, *Breathing Room*, a collection of linked stories. Art has been an important part of Mary's healing from breast cancer.

Although Mary minored in painting in college and studied with different teachers, it wasn't until 1999, when she began studying pastel painting, that she really understood the power of color and light. She became a student of full-color seeing, attending classes with teacher and artist Susan Sarback at The School of Light and Color in Fair Oaks, California. For more about Mary and her work, visit *www.marycarroll moore.com*.

Rachel Naomi Remen, M.D. is one of the earliest pioneers in the mind/body holistic health movement and the first to recognize the role of the spirit in health and the recovery from illness. She is Co-Founder and Medical Director of the Commonweal Cancer Help Program featured in the Bill Moyers PBS series, *Healing and the Mind,* and she has cared for people with cancer and their families for almost 30 years. She is also a nationally recognized medical reformer and educator who sees the practice of medicine as a spiritual path. In recognition of her work, she has received several honorary degrees and has been invited to teach in medical schools and hospitals throughout the country. Her ground-breaking holistic curricula enable physicians at all levels of training to remember their calling and strengthen their commitment to serve life.

Dr. Remen is Clinical Professor of Family and Community Medicine at the UCSF School of Medicine and Director of the innovative UCSF course *The Healer's Art,* which was recently featured in *US News & World Report*. She is also the founder and Director of the Institute for the Study of Health and Illness, a ten-year-old professional development program for graduate physicians.

She is the author of the *New York Times* best seller *Kitchen Table Wisdom: Stories That Heal*, Riverhead Books, 1996. Her newest book, *My Grandfather's Blessings: Stories of Strength, Refuge and Belonging,* 2000 (Riverhead Books), is a national bestseller. As a master story-teller and public speaker, she has spoken to thousands of people throughout the country, reminding them of the power of their humanity and the ability to use their lives to make a difference. Dr. Remen has a 48-year personal history of Crohn's disease, and her work is a unique blend of the viewpoint of physician and patient.

Judy Vashti Persad, a Soul who loves to dance with words, gets lost in finding the perfect shot, spends too much time daydreaming in a song, and enjoys the night time for its silence and intensity, yet sometimes spends it listening to music with headphones on. She currently lives in Toronto and can be reached at *jvpersad@hotmail.com*.

Judy Conlin Prang resides in Kingston, Ontario with her husband, Cal. She is Area Manager for a major financial institution, and she volunteers her time on the Board of Directors of The Elizabeth Fry Society of Kingston, an organization that supports women in conflict, or in danger of coming into conflict, with the law. Building on her communication, facilitation and motivational skills, Judy, the mother of two grown daughters and grandmother of five, has only recently committed to fulfilling her true vocation of being a writer. She is currently working on her first book and can be reached at *judyprang@hotmail.com*.

Laura Reave, Ph.D. has been a writer, editor, and English professor for fifteen years. Her current research interest is spiritual leadership, and she has an article forthcoming on this topic in the journal *Leadership Quarterly*. She also has particular interest in spiritual poetry. She is proud to serve as the editor for *Conscious Women – Conscious Lives Book Two*. She can be reached at *lreave@ody.ca*.

Glenna Salsbury, CSP, CPAE, Speaker Hall of Fame, graduated from Northwestern University in Evenston, Illinois, obtained her master's degree from UCLA, and sixteen years later, earned a master's in theology from Fuller Seminary. In 1980, Glenna founded her own company, which provides keynote presentations and personal growth seminars. Glenna is past president of the National Speakers Association. In her personal life, Glenna was married to the late Jim Salsbury, a former Detroit Lion and Green Bay Packer. She has three daughters and five grandchildren. Call, email or write to obtain her powerful six-pack tape album entitled Passion, Prayer and Purpose and/or her book, *The Art of the Fresh Start*. She can be reached at *Ispeak4U@aol.com*. 9228 N. 64th Place, Paradise Valley, AZ 85253 or call 480-483-7732.

Janine Gwendoline Smith is a Renaissance Artist whose love for life fuels her passionate creativity. Defying definition and category, Janine reaches out to share rare sensitivity and vision as Spirit moves her. She pursues excellence in her disciplines of singing, songwriting, painting, design, clay sculpture, poetry, acting and T'ai Chi. Janine draws inspiration from such people as the dedicated Viggo Mortensen and the fearless Karl Lagerfield. Janine's birth in South Africa and subsequent travels (living in four countries, on three continents by the time she was five) exposed her to many influences.

In 2002, Janine released her first solo CD, "LOVE LIVES INSIDE," and she has one BRAVO! Video from that CD to date. Janine's music is eclectic, international, and universal, with exquisite arrangements. Her vocal style has been compared to the likes of Sarah Brightman, Kate Bush, Ella Fitzgerald, and Elaine Paul. When asked what kind of music she performs, Janine responds, "Beautiful Music." She also loves jazz standards, and she can torch a song with her fluidic range. Janine's path is an infinite quest to unfold to a greater and greater expression of the Divine Potential within.

Christine Switzer was a photographer at the time of her daughter's struggle with anorexia, mostly in fashion photography. She later left the fashion industry and began photographing pregnant women. Her work has been featured on the TV channel, The Life Network. Chris also does family portraits and wedding photography, and she loves to ride her horse Oz. Her email is *cswitzer@rogers.com*.

Claudette Viau was born in Montreal, Canada. After studying in the sciences, she became an acupuncturist. Claudette is a pioneer in alternative medicine and psychology. She now lives in Ottawa, where she continues to work in the field of holistic medicine, and where she is deeply involved in palliative care. Claudette's vision is to combine healing methods with sounds, music, and visualization to bring peace and harmony. You can contact her at *cviauacup@sympatico.ca*.

Marianne Williamson is an internationally acclaimed author and lecturer. She has published eight books, four of which – including the mega best seller *A Return to Love* and the newly-released *Everyday Grace* – have been No. 1 New York Times' best sellers. Her titles also include *Illuminata*, *A Woman's Worth*, and *Healing the Soul of America*. She also edited *Imagine: What American Could Be in the 21st Century*, a compilation of essays by some of America's most visionary thinkers. Ms Williamson has been a popular guest on numerous television programs such as Oprah, Larry King Live, Good Morning America, and Charlie Rose. Marianne Williamson has lectured professionally since 1983. In 1989, she founded Project Angel Food, a meals-on-wheels program that serves homebound people with AIDS in the Los Angeles area. Today, Project Angel Food serves over 1,000 people daily. Ms Williamson also co-founded the Global Renaissance Alliance (GRA), a worldwide network of peace activists. The mission of the GRA is to harness the power of nonviolence as a social force for good. Her latest book, *Everyday Grace: Having Hope, Finding Forgiveness and Making Miracles*, was published by Riverhead Books (Nov. 2002) and quickly reached #1 on the New York Times' Best-Seller List (December 2002). Ms Williamson's new book, *The Gift of Change: Spiritual Guidance for a Radically New Life*, was released from Harper Collins, November 2004. For more about Marianne Williamson, visit *www.marianne.com*.

Permissions

Life is a Gift, Reprinted by permission of Sybil Barbour
© 2004 Sybil Barbour

Once at Big Lake, Reprinted by permission of Laura Reave
© 2004 Laura Reave

A *Circle of Friends: Part Two*, Reprinted by permission of Arlene
Forbes © 2004 Arlene Forbes

The Road Less Traveled, Reprinted by permission of Deborah
Davis © 2004 Deborah Davis

Starting to Choose, Reprinted by permission of Georgina Cannon
© 2004 Georgina Cannon

Journey Back to Life,Reprinted by permission of Sheri Kaplan
© 2004 Sheri Kaplan

Grappling With Destiny, Reprinted by permission of Jim Bronson
© 1994 Merrily Bronson

My Last Journey, Reprinted by permission of Ruth Edgett
© 2004 Ruth Edgett

Why I Lived, and Why I Died, Reprinted by permission of Judy
Prang © 2004 Judy Prang

A *Taste of Death*, Reprinted by permission of Jo Leonard
© 2004 Jo Leonard

A *Prayer To Know One's Calling*, Reprinted by permission of
Erin Davis © 2004 Erin Davis

Opening My Eyes to the Light, Reprinted by permission of
Marianne Bai-Woo © 2004 Marianne Bai-Woo

A *Lion's Heart*, Reprinted by permission of Cathleen Fillmore © 2004 Cathleen Fillmore

Remembering Eric, Reprinted by permission of Tracy Clausell-Alexander © 2004 Tracy Clausell-Alexander

The Red Chair Experiment, Reprinted by permission of Shelley Hyndman © 2004 Shelley Hyndman

The Visit, Reprinted by permission of Carole Matthews © 2004 Carole Matthews

The Littlest Angel, Reprinted by permission of Brenda Mallory © 1999 Brenda Mallory, from *Chicken Soup for the Canadian Soul*

The Gift of Miracles, Reprinted by permission of Cynthia Brian © 2004 Cynthia Brian

One Small Miracle, Reprinted by permission of Jo Leonard © 2004 Jo Leonard

A *Garden in Brooklyn*, Reprinted by permission of Laura Reave © 2004 Laura Reave

The Hug, Reprinted by permission of Barbara Allport © 2004 Barbara Allport

A *Pact Made in Heaven*, Reprinted by permission of Sandra Irvine © 2004 Sandra Irvine

Contemplation on Monet's Water Lilies, Reprinted by permission of Laura Reave © 2004 Laura Reave

Coming Home to Oz, Reprinted by permission of Christine Switzer © 2004 Christine Switzer

Glenna's Goal Book, Reprinted by permission of Glenna Salsbury © Glenna Salsbury. Originally printed in *Chicken Soup for the Soul*

Shield of Protection, Reprinted by permission of Judy Vashti Persad © 2005 Judy Vashti Persad

A *New Way Of Seeing*, Reprinted by permission of Andrea Leake © 2004 Andrea Leake

Magical Love Story, Reprinted by permission of Claudette Viau © 2004 Claudette Viau

Mastery, Reprinted by permission of Janine Gwendoline Smith © 1995 (All Rights Reserved) SOCAN, © 2001 Beyond Fifth Plane Music (All Rights Reserved) SOCAN

The Good Girl, Reprinted by permission of Kati Alexandra © 2004 Kati Alexandra

Santa Fe Dreamin', Reprinted by permission of Alissa M. Lukara © 2005 Alissa M. Lukara

Healing My Perceptions, by Marianne Williamson from *A Return to Love* by Marianne Williamson, pages 202-206. Copyright © 1992 by Marianne Williamson. Portions reprinted from a Course in Miracles copyright © 1975 by Foundation for Inner Peace Inc. All chapter openings are from a COURSE IN MIRACLES.

"The Emperor's New Clothes" by Rachel Remen, M.D., from KITCHEN TABLE WISDOM by Rachel Naomi Remen, M.D., copyright © 1996 by Rachel Naomi Remen, M.D. Used by permission of Riverhead Books, an imprint of Penguin Group (USA) Inc.

IF YOU WERE REALLY IMPORTANT ... © 1992, 2004 Susan Jeffers, Ph.D. from *Life is Huge! www.susanjeffers.com*

A Prayer to Know One's Calling Copyright © 2001 Catholic Doors Ministry (Used with permission.) Copyright © 1995, December 1. # 659.

WHITE KNIGHT'S
"REMARKABLE WOMEN" SERIES

Sharing MS

This informative book by the author and two women friends with Multiple Sclerosis, is a beacon of common sense lighting the way of those who have MS or suspect they may be afflicted, as well as being helpful to family, friends and health professionals. Read the book then call the MS Society Chapter in your local telephone book for information about your concerns regarding Multiple Sclerosis. ISBN 0-9730949-7-4 218 pages PB US $13.95 Cdn $19.95

The Unusual Life and Times of Nancy Ford-Inman

This story is about a most remarkable woman who contributed so much to Britain's literature, the theatre, media and the war effort in spite of a major physical handicap. Badly crippled by Cerebral Palsy at an early age, she fought her way to become the author of almost 60 romantic novels and journalistic endeavors too numerous to count.
ISBN 0-9730949-8-2 238 pages PB
US $13.95 Cdn $19.95

To order, contact one of the distributors shown on the copyright page or be in touch with the book store nearest to you.

BOOKS BY WHITE KNIGHT PUBLICATIONS

ADOPTION (Gay)
A Swim Against The Tide
    – David R.I. McKinstry

BIOGRAPHY
The Life and Times of Nancy
Ford-Inman – Nancy Erb Kee

HEALTH
Prescription for Patience
    – Dr. Kevin J Leonard

HUMOUR
An Innkeeper's Discretion Book
    One & An Innkeeper's
    Discretion Book Two
    – David R.I. McKinstry

INSPIRATION
Conscious Women / Conscious
    Lives Book One
Conscious Women / Conscious
    Lives Book Two
    – Darlene Montgomery
Happiness: Use It or Lose It
    – Rev. Dr. David "Doc"
    Loomis
How I Became Father to
    1000 Children
    – Rev. Dr. John S. Niles
Sharing MS (Multiple Sclerosis) –
    Linda Ironside
Sue Kenney's My Camino
    – Sue Kenney

PERSONAL FINANCES
Don't Borrow $Money$ Until You
    Read This Book
    – Paul E Counter

POETRY
Loveplay – Joe Fromstein
    and Linda Stitt
Two Voices / A Circle of Love
    – Serena Williamson Adams

POLITICS AND HISTORY
Prophets of Violence / Prophets of
    Peace – Dr. K. Sohail
Turning Points – Ray Argyle

SELF-HELP
Love, Sex and Marriage
    – Dr. K. Sohail/Bette Davis
The Art of Living in Your Green
    Zone
    – Dr. K. Sohail
The Art of Loving in Your Green
    Zone
    – Dr. K. Sohail
The Art of Working in Your Green
    Zone
    – Dr. K. Sohail/Bette Davis

TRUE CRIME – POLICE
10-45 Spells Death
    – Kathy McCormack Carter
Life on Homicide
    - Former Police Chief Bill
    McCormack
The Myth of The Chosen One
    – Dr. K. Sohail

RECOMMENDED READING
FROM OTHER PUBLISHERS

HISTORY
An Amicable Friendship (Canadiana) – Jan Th. J. Krijff

RELIGION
From Islam to Secular Humanism – Dr. K. Sohail

BIOGRAPHY
Gabriel's Dragon – Arch Priest Fr. Antony Gabriel

EPIC POETRY
Pro Deo – Prof. Ronald Morton Smith